Donut Dollies

in Vietnam:

Baby-Blue Dresses
& OD Green

Nancy Smoyer

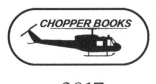

2017

ISBN 978-0692878002

Book design, layout and formatting by Pingo Press

Printed in the United States

First edition - 2017

Published by Chopper Books
   chopperbooksdd@gmail.com

Front cover – Nancy Smoyer in front of Cu Chi Clubmobile sign with office to the right and our hooch behind

All proceeds from this book will be donated to the Semper Fi Fund, an A+ rated charity which provides resources and lifetime support for wounded, critically ill and injured service members, veterans and their families. <www.semperfifund.org>

Table of Contents

Table of Contents

Part II – The Aftermath

Preface

This memoir began 50 years ago with my first letter home to my parents from Vietnam in April 1967. After I got back home a year later, I read every book that came out about Vietnam until there got to be too many and I was finally sated 20 years later. Around that time I discovered email groups of Vietnam veterans which opened a floodgate of writing, giving me a place to share my memories and to hear others'. These exchanges caused me to think about my relationship to the veteran community and how I could relate to these men whom I had known as boys. It also gave me a place to talk about the pain of losing my younger brother in Vietnam which I hadn't been able to do before.

This book is those letters and tapes home, as well as the email exchanges and musings. The letters and tapes are identified as such. The emails are in a slightly bolder font. Some are written to the email groups of primarily male Vietnam veterans (wearers of olive drab green) and some to a group of Donut Dollies (wearers of baby blue dresses). The tone for the most part is informal—written to comrades who share the same background and so need little explanation.

Although both the men and the women shared many of the same experiences, no one can speak for all of us. The experiences of the girls varied greatly depending on the time period they were there, which unit they served with, and the various daily events of life in Vietnam as one of 627 women in a sea of green. As women, we can never understand how it feels to walk through the jungle, pull night guard duty on the perimeter or sit on a firebase waiting. But we experienced fear and the real possibility of death. We shared the heat and humidity, the foreignness of the country, the quandary of our involvement there, and the return home. We shared the losses then and the coming together now.

This offering is for those who were there, for those who loved them then and now, and for those who hope to gain some understanding of what it was like for one person, a Donut Dollie.

Red Cross Supplemental Recreation Activities Overseas

Over the course of almost seven years, from September 1965 to May 1972, 627 young women, all college graduates, served in South Vietnam in the Supplemental Recreation Activities Overseas (SRAO) program, known informally as Red Cross recreation workers, and even more informally by our nickname, Donut Dollies. The units were throughout South Vietnam, opening and closing depending on troop movement and other factors. Each unit varied in size from four to twelve girls, with the largest number of women in country at one time being 109 in 1969. Many units had recreation centers, while others focused on doing daily runs around the camp or flying or driving to forward LZs (Landing Zones) and fire bases to bring our "program" to the men.

For military operations the country was divided into Corps Tactical Zones, also referred to as Military Regions. The map on the following pages shows the locations of the SRAO units within each of the four Corps Zones. The locations for Red Cross units were located on the map by Bobbi McDaniel Stephens, fellow Donut Dollie.

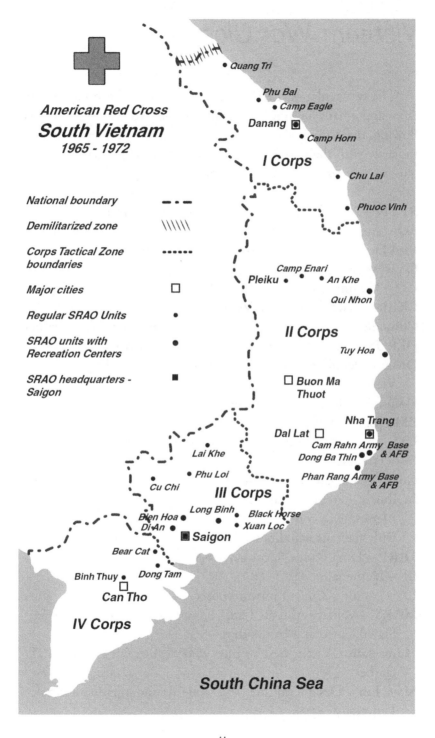

American Red Cross
South Vietnam
1965 - 1972

National boundary	— · —
Demilitarized zone	\\\\\\
Corps Tactical Zone boundaries	······
Major cities	□
Regular SRAO Units	•
SRAO units with Recreation Centers	●
SRAO headquarters - Saigon	■

• Quang Tri

Phu Bai
• Camp Eagle

Danang ◉

I Corps

• Camp Horn

• Chu Lai

• Phuoc Vinh

Camp Enari
Pleiku •   • • An Khe

Qui Nhon

II Corps

Tuy Hoa

□ Buon Ma Thuot

Nha Trang
Dal Lat □   ◉
Cam Rahn Army Base & AFB
Dong Ba Thin ●●
Phan Rang Army Base & AFB

Lai Khe •

• Phu Loi

• Cu Chi

III Corps

Long Binh •   • Black Horse
Bien Hoa •
Di An •   • Xuan Loc
■ Saigon

Bear Cat •

Binh Thuy • Dong Tam
□
Can Tho

IV Corps

South China Sea

vii

Vietnam War Glossary

The vernacular of the Vietnam war found in this book's letters, tapes and emails has not been changed. Also, to keep the narrative flowing, definitions have not been inserted into the text. Since familiarity with these terms is helpful in following the narrative, this glossary has been located at the front of the book.

AFVN – Armed (later American) Forces Radio Vietnam
AO – Area of Operation
Bird Dog – Fixed-wing, two-seater observational plane
C-rats (rations) – Canned food for use in the field
CO – Commanding Officer
Charlie – Viet Cong, from VC—Victor Charlie
Chinook – Large, twin-engine, tandem rotor heavy-lift helicopter
DEROS – Date of Expected Return from Overseas
DMZ – Demilitarized Zone at border of North and South Vietnam
Donut 6 – Head Donut Dollie of unit
EM – Enlisted Man
ETS – Estimate Time of Separation from military
FB – Firebase
Gook – Derogatory slang for Vietnamese people
In Touch – Program started by Friends of the Vietnam Veterans Memorial to connect families who lost someone in Vietnam with veterans who knew them
LRRP – Long Range Reconnaissance Patrol
LT – Lieutenant
LZ – Landing Zone of forward posts
MARS – Military Affiliate Radio Station. Used to call home via Signal Corps and ham radios
Mama-sans – Vietnamese women who cleaned our hooches and clothes
Maya Lin – Designer of the Wall while an undergraduate at Yale University

MedCap – Medical Civil Action Program

Medevac – Medical evacuation

NCO – Non-Commissioned Officer

NSA – Naval Support Activity

NVA – North Vietnamese Army

OD – Olive Drab—green color of military uniforms

OJT – On the Job Training

Otter – Single-engine, high-wing, propeller-driven, short take-off and landing plane with seating for about 10

PTSD – Post-traumatic Stress Disorder

REMF – Rear Echelon Military Force; derogatorily Rear Echelon Mother F____

R&R – Rest and Relaxation/Recuperation

Round Eyes – Term used for non-Asian woman

RTO – Radio Telephone Operator who carried his unit's radio in the field

Sappers – Highly-trained enemy soldiers who infiltrated bases

Stand Down – Stand downs in Vietnam were times when the men came in from the field to their base camp, giving them a time to regroup and take care of various needs. Since the early 1980s, Stand Downs have been organized in the States as 1-day to 3-day events to provide supplies and services to veterans in need.

Strac – Smart, sharp, well-prepared

TAD – Temporary Assigned Duty, Marine-speak for TDY

TDY – Temporary Duty

Tet – Surprise attacks by the VC and NVA throughout South Vietnam, beginning on January 30, 1968, Vietnamese New Year

UD – Unit Director, same-same Donut 6

USO – United Service Organization

VC – Viet Cong

VVA – Vietnam Veterans of America

VVAW – Vietnam Veterans Against the War

Wall – Vietnam Veterans Memorial in Washington, DC

White Mice – South Vietnamese police who wore white uniforms

Zippo – Cigarette lighter

Part I

Vietnam

What's a girl like you doing in a place like this?

The seeds of my interest in working with GIs began early and have continued throughout my life. These emails written to a veteran email group describe the steps along the way.

When people ask why I went to Vietnam, my short answer is "Because the guys had to be there and I wanted to do what I could to help." Short and sweet—and honest besides. But the roots go much farther back.

It all began when I was around 10 years old. I was raised in Princeton, NJ, in a family where there was little thought of serving in the military and hardly anybody went to Vietnam. My uncles had been in the service in WWII, but not my father who worked on the War Board in Washington, D.C.

My family had a coffee table book called *Life Goes to War*, and as I looked at the photographs of the tired and dirty soldiers, I became curious about them and war. Then in my mid-teens I read *All Quiet on the Western Front*, a novel written by a German veteran in WWI. Interestingly, when I reread the book after Vietnam, I found that the words spoken by these German soldiers about the effects of the war on them could have been spoken by Vietnam veterans. Reading this book caused me to think not only about our American soldiers but those of the "enemy" as well, and I became more curious about war in general.

My first actual encounter with GIs occurred on the 8th-grade class trip to DC in 1957. There's a motel across the street from Fort Myer outside of DC and, as it happens, we stayed at that motel. I went to a small girls' school in Princeton, so there were

21 girls staying right across the street from a major army base. Needless to say, we soon discovered each other. So whenever we weren't touring the Lincoln Memorial or the FBI or whatever other sight, we were running across the 4-lane road, talking to the GIs through the fence. At our class reunions, we all remember that experience with great clarity. It was my first exposure to genuine GIs—and look where it got me.......

A later email continues the story in an effort to explain my "journey" to Vietnam.

While spending my junior year of college in Bordeaux, France, my friends and I often went to the USO during the day to eat American chocolate, smoke American cigarettes and listen to American rock-n-roll music. Occasionally we talked to the men, but mostly it was just a chance to have a refuge in a semi-hostile country.

After I graduated college in 1965, I went on a round-the-world trip for 15 months, traveling and working in England, Israel and Australia. The war was revving up, and everywhere I went I heard negative comments about our involvement. The only exception was Australia where men and women were beginning to go too. I was in a pub one evening where there was a party for a bloke who was on his way to Vietnam. I felt a sense of guilt that he was going to fight "our" war.

During this time, I didn't have clear opinions about our involvement in Vietnam, but what became clearer and clearer as I traveled in foreign countries was that reminders of home were a soothing balm. I decided that if our men had to be there, whether they wanted to be or not, I would go and do what I could to make it better for them, to bring them a touch of home. I also would finally be able to find out what war was really like.

So at the end of my wanderings, almost as soon as I arrived home in early 1967, I started investigating ways to go to Vietnam. I didn't care about the politics of our involvement and I tried very hard to stay apolitical while I was there. I looked into

Special Services, USO and others, but when I learned that the Red Cross got us as far forward as women were allowed to go, except for journalists, that sealed it. I interviewed, was accepted and went, all within three months of returning home. I was off again, this time for a year in Vietnam—which I still refer to as the best year of my life...and the worst.

When I was going through my mother's papers, I found the following letter from the Area Director, Personnel Services, ARC, April 10, 1967. I like the acknowledgment in the last sentence of the contribution the families too are making. And I can certainly agree with the mention of the lasting (and new) friendships we made.

Dear Mr. and Mrs. Smoyer:

We would like to take this opportunity to let you know that we are pleased to have your daughter join our Supplemental Recreation Activities Overseas program, and to assure you that we are most interested in her health and happiness while she is overseas. These girls [I was almost 25 years old] work together as a close-knit group and form lasting friendships. For the girls, the time overseas passes very quickly, and they are full of enthusiasm on their return to the United States. We feel certain that this will be a very enriching and rewarding experience in Nancy's life.

If at any time you need information regarding your daughter, we suggest you contact the Red Cross chapter in your community. You will be interested to know that during their training course in Washington, D.C., the girls are encouraged to write home frequently.

We are most appreciative of the service contribution you have made through Nancy.

Sincerely,

Criterion for a Red Cross Girl

2

I'm not sure how or when in my tour I came upon this description of the qualities found in a "typical" Red Cross girl. I seem to have thought it would help my parents understand not only a little bit about our job but also about myself, so I sent it to them with my note attached that reads, "I'm sending this thing about the Red Cross girl—it's really perfect. Some days or hours recently I haven't wanted to talk to or see anyone, and then a friend or an especially happy, cute face pops up and I forget how sour I feel until he leaves or somebody interrupts asking for ping pong balls, writing papers, string, telephone – you name it."

Criterion for a Red Cross Girl
(with apologies to the author of Criterion for a GI)

After the security of childhood and before the security of marriage, we find the Red Cross girl. Red Cross girls are found everywhere: in the Center, on the perimeter, in the air, on your secured ground, in love, on leave, in a constantly enthusiastic state, out of sorts, in bars and behind bars (coffee, that is), in the swing of things (new girl), out of the running (short timer), in debt. Red Cross girls come in assorted sizes, weights and states of sobriety, misery and confusion. Men love them, fathers tolerate them, the military supports them and somehow they seem to get along with each other.

A Red Cross girl is lazy with a deck of cards, a millionaire without a cent, brave without a grain of sense. She is the protector of America with the latest copy of a program format in her hand. A Red Cross girl is a composite to the GI: she has the energy of a turtle or a beaver, the brains of an idiot or a wise man, the sincerity of a liar or a saint. She is sly as a fox and has the stories of a combat veteran. She has the appetite of an elephant, the aspirations of a Clara Barton on the morale battlefield. And when she wants something it's usually: a 3-day weekend away from her unit, a cigarette, five dollars, a button for her uniform, an ice cold beer, hot water, a black magic marker, hot drink cups, an addition to her center, a new coffee pot, just one more mobile stop, a visit to the forward area, a kind word, a moment's peace. She dislikes: superior officers, hard core NCO's, demanding EM's, getting up to face a new day when she's fresh out of smiles, the caloric content of Army chow, C-123's, the day before pay check day when they get all the goodies in the PX, dirt (dust or mud), a million and one regulations.

No man can tame her, no woman can beat her. She is reliable, responsible, and indestructible. No one else can write so seldom, yet think of her loved ones so much. No one else can get so much of out of: mail, civilian clothes, a good book, an intellectual conversation, or a stolen moment completely alone—anything that reinforces her individual identity. A Red Cross girl is a gay, magical creature. You can lock her out of your forward area battlefields, but not out of your heart.

Coming Into Country

3

Letter. April 29, 1967, Saigon

In Saigon after a 21-hour plane ride. As you know, I've been in some pretty dirty, messy cities, but this beats all. All the houses look like shacks and are beat up; the main roads are incredibly narrow. My picture of Saigon was wide streets with the American Embassy on a huge square with rubble around and bombed buildings. Instead there's just general mess. The place is mobbed with Hondo-type bikes and regular bikes. The whole town and especially this hotel smell musty. We're staying in American bachelor quarters (combination hotel and coed YWCA—the Rex). The people are tiny and scary—I think each one is a VC with a hand grenade. There's a notice downstairs that says, "Grenade attacks are on the increase. Don't congregate at bus stops." I tell you this not to scare you, although I know it will (it scares me), but just so you'll know about it. The place is so mobbed with Vietnamese and American soldiers, and there are two Aussie Jeeps parked outside. It all seems terribly foreign, dirty, depressing and ugly, even though I know I've been in very similar places. It must be awful for the other girls. I think I'll get used to it before long.

The plane trip was OK. We went by the northern route, Alaska and Japan, but got into Alaska at 2:00 am so saw nothing—quelle disappointment. Also saw nothing in Japan. I slept 12 hours straight and read the rest of the time and talked to a couple of guys. The night we left we went out early to the base in San Francisco and checked in and went to the Officers' Club. Talked to an Air Force guy who had just gotten back that day—had been stationed at Cam Ranh Bay, and said it would be a terrible place for me to go because it's so civilized, secure and easy. I've got to get stationed in the toolies.

After we left Japan, we were rerouted and delayed because of military action over the Saigon area, so we landed four hours late at a different air base but I've heard nothing about what happened. But when they first told us we were changing course, bad thoughts started coming, like what if they shoot at us. I now have a very small idea of what a pilot on a mission feels. As things go on, I'll know more what the soldier feels by experiencing it myself, which is the only way I seem to be able to understand things. As we first sighted Vietnam and came in to land, everyone on the plane got real quiet. I don't know what they were thinking, but I was thinking that some of those guys weren't going to make it back—they would die with blood and mud all over them. Sounds corny and melodramatic, but when these feelings are happening to you, you know all the stuff that's written isn't just tripe.

Two days later. In two days my impressions have settled down a little. It's still very depressing, crowded, messy, and I find there are some widish roads, and it could be half-way decent without the hordes of people.

Last night we went to an officers' mess (as we had the night before) in a hotel and had drinks and then decided to go eat in a Vietnamese place. I was very glad to eat in another place because there had been rumors flying around that the Rex Hotel was going to be bombed at 9:00. All sorts of different people had heard the rumor before going, and about half the Vietnamese waitresses hadn't shown up, which was supposed to be the true test if it was true. Of course, nothing happened, but I don't like tempting fate any more than necessary. The Vietnamese dinner I had was cannelloni!—but very good. Haven't seen any Aussie soldiers yet, which is sad.

The Cav

4

The 1st Cav was my first assignment and, as the saying goes, you never get over your first love. It was special to me for many reasons— their enormous pride in their division, all those choppers, and the big yellow patch that we proudly wore on our shoulder. In Vietnam the official name was 1st Cavalry Division (Airmobile) when the horses of the original Cavalry became helicopters—many many helicopters— which were a joy to ride in. I was with the Cav from the end of April in 1967 until the end of July—three too-short months.

Letter. April 29, Saigon

We just found out our assignments, and joy of all joys, I got exactly the place I want—An Khe with the 1st Cavalry. I'm so excited and happy about it. It's a center/clubmobile, i.e., so I do both, and we go on our runs in helicopters, which is great! I will be the 8th girl—they've just moved out of tents into I'm not sure what. I leave tonight by plane—must be at the airport at 4:30 in the morning, so no sleep tonight, but I couldn't anyway.

Letter. May 2, An Khe

This probably won't be very coherent because I'm too hot to think—my brain has melted. Fortunately, evenings are cool—even sleep with blankets. This is my third day here. I flew up in a box-car-type plane, C-130, and I got to sit up front with the pilots. It was really cool because they gave me earphones, and we all talked to each other on them, and they showed me places as we flew over them. At one place where we were going to land (we had landed twice before An Khe) they reported artillery fire from the airport so we had to change course slightly, but of course never saw any.

The base itself is huge—much bigger and more spread out than I pictured. We have two layers of barbed wire around our billet and 2 guards at night—well protected.

Letter. May 11, An Khe

When I first got here, I was too hot to eat at all—about a half a meal a day, but now I'm back to two and will regain the weight I've lost. Fortunately I've gotten somewhat used to the heat. At first I really thought I couldn't last the year.

In the interim between these letters, I wrote about our living conditions (Hooches), daily lives (Alerts, Programming) and my feelings about the men and the war. Here I continue with my feelings about the Cav and my sadness at leaving them which continued throughout my tour.

Letter. July 23, An Khe

I have some really bad news. I'm being transferred to Danang in four days. Our unit is so screwed up and disorganized. When I leave there will be four girls who have been here one to three months (right now I've been here longer than anyone else), three who are brand new in country and two who are brand new to the unit. It's almost impossible to operate effectively like that. All sorts of little things have been going wrong, like no supplies (cards, wrapping paper, tape, etc.); our Clubmobile stops are getting messed up; so many of the Cav guys are going home—all the guys I knew when I first came. In that respect, I'm almost glad to be leaving now because most of my friends have gone, although I hate to leave the ones I have.

I hate to leave the Cav—no more trips to the field on choppers, seeing the guys all grubby in their bunkers, no more rustic country living (we live in the city of Danang), leaving my friends just as I was really feeling adjusted and able to be helpful to the unit; no more big yellow Cav patch on my sleeve. But Danang is the one other place I want to go to—to see what Billy [my brother] will be like, and just to be with the wonderful Marines.

On the radio last night (my weekly radio DJ show), I had to say goodbye, and I darn near started to cry over the air. Fortunately, I waited to say goodbye until the end of the show, because I couldn't talk for about two minutes after I told the Cav goodbye.

Letter. Aug. 28, Danang

I got them to delay my transfer [from An Khe] three days because we told them I was really needed for the next few days because the new girls were coming in later than expected. Really I wanted to stay because a battalion of my favorite unit that I keep telling you about was coming in from the field for the first time since last November and they wanted two of us to serve cake and coffee to them. So of course I was dying to see them come and so I managed to get them to let me stay. It really made a lot of difference to have these last few days because it gave me just a few extra days to adjust to the idea.

The day before I left a favorite friend of mine from that unit that came in—he's the guy I wrote you about who was in reform school for so long and who is such a good artist—well, he had just gotten back from R&R and while he was there he got me a crucifix on a chain which he gave me. He's Catholic and I hated to tell him my thoughts on religion so I wear it now with the crucifix at the back because I would feel like such a hypocrite if I wore it where people could see it. But it was one of the really sweet things guys do for us over here and it really makes me feel good.

Did I ever tell you about my friend Skip? He's a Negro guy who I got to know pretty well. He has a really funny off-beat sense of humor which first made me notice him and then I got to talk to him lots in the center. He was pretty interesting although some of his stories got kind of long and drawn out, but I think I could have learned a lot if I'd gotten to know him better but then I left.

One more thing about the Cav before I left. I had a Center program which was supposed to be a fashion show and it was really fun. We started out by dressing up a guy in a funny cloth mini-skirt and then putting make-up all over his face – lipstick, eyebrow pencil, etc., etc.. Then we had a "real" fashion show where three of us put on some of our wilder clothes (like my tent dress and paper dress) and modeled them. We also did funny things like wearing fatigues and a mini Red Cross uniform. It was really fun and the guys get a real charge out of seeing real round-eyes in real dresses, not just uniforms.

I still get really upset whenever I think about the Cav. In fact last night I was with a guy I've been dating quite a bit lately and he asked me, just what is it about the Cav that I'm so hung up about, and I just started to cry right there and couldn't explain. Nobody, not even the other girls over here, can understand what it is about the Cav unless they've been there.

Letter. Aug. 30, Danang

I nearly forgot to tell you about the most exciting thing that has happened to me since I got to Danang. A week ago I had a two-day weekend and so I went back down to An Khe for a visit. Needless to say, it was fun. I was really lucky because a lot of my favorite friends were there and not in the field. It was also great to see my two favorite girlfriends—the three of us used to have the funniest times.

A bunch of us had dinner at the general's mess and I was guest of honor because we always go there before we leave and I didn't have a chance. And guess who the general was—Tolson. He never eats in the mess at An Khe because he's always in the field. I think this is the second time practically since he's been there, but I was really lucky that he was in that day. So he gave me a certificate making me an honorary sky-trooper (what we call the Cav men) and a Cav medallion and crest. Then I had to make a speech and I said about three words and nearly started to cry again. I felt so stupid.

Letter. Oct. 8, Danang

I got a letter from a guy in the Cav just a few days ago. He's from my favorite unit in all the Cav, but the funny thing is I can't remember him at all. And yet he wrote me this unbelievably sweet letter. The rewards from this job are impossible to explain.

11

Hello, Nancy!

Well, I sure hope you don't mind me writing because you sure are remembered by the Co C, 2/7. You may not remember me, but you came out to LZ Judy and I was in the tower at the time and I also talked to you many times at the Red Cross.

A few of us from the 2/7th went to the Red Cross to see you, but when the girls there told me that you had left I was really sorry to hear it for now we here miss you very much and I hope you will come back to see us sometime soon.

Also, how do you like it where you are and you must have a lot of friends there, but never will you have as many friends as you do in the 2/7th. Nancy, if at any time you ever need anything, please just write and we back here will do everything we can for you. You are the only girl, you see, that has always been very sweet to the 1st Cav and like I said, you will always be thought of and well, I guess all I can say is take care and may God bless you wherever you may go.

Your friends, 2/7th,

PFC Michael G.

Tape. Pre-Christmas #2, Cu Chi

I started making tapes to my parents, rather than writing letters, about halfway through my tour using a small, very basic tape recorder that had been sent to me by an organization in my home town.

I was still mourning the Cav in this tape I sent in December.

I'll never forget the Cav and how I felt when I was there. The other night I was standing outside an officers' club where we go for parties, just looking at bunkers and houses and choppers and stuff, and I was thinking how I would have felt if I had been in An Khe in the same situation. I know how I would have felt. I would have gotten this great wonderful feeling of proud to be there and to be with the Cav and here I just sort of felt, you know, here I am. Oh well, I'm going to try to forget about the Cav, but I can't.

Alerts

5

My first alert happened my first night at my first unit, An Khe, and they continued in various places and in various forms throughout my tour. Tet in January-February 1968 at Cu Chi was the most threatening and long-lasting, but that story comes later.

Letter. May 2, An Khe

My first night here we had an alert which means that the enemy was moving around the camp, but all the helicopters went up, etc., etc. and nothing happened that we saw. But it was a pretty exciting first night since we all put on our fatigues and about 10 people told me what to do if we were mortared, i.e., dive under the bed with helmet and be flat, and about 10 more told me not to be afraid. Of course I was but I got bored with nothing happening so went to bed (after two hours sleep the night before having gotten up at 3:00 the night before to get the plane to An Khe).

There's really very little danger because of the way the mortars explode—out in an arc, not straight out—so you're okay under something and also because we're about three miles from the airstrip which is what they're aiming for.

Letter. May 11, An Khe

The other night at 4:00 am we had a practice alert. I happened to be awake scratching mosquito bites when sirens started going off. We all started running around, putting on fatigues, not knowing where to go; and then we called somebody, discovered it was a practice, and went back to bed. During all the fuss, which lasted about five minutes, I wasn't scared at all—just busily getting dressed and finding out what was going on. It's strange because I would have expected to be scared.

Letter. July 14, An Khe

I went out with a guy I had been out with once before. We went to a club and were sitting with another man talking about medals and how worthless they're becoming, especially bronze stars and especially for officers because anyone can get one. (I found out later this guy I was with, a lieutenant, has gotten a silver star.) All of the sudden the sirens started to go off—an alert. We raced for a bunker—it was a command bunker so there were cots, etc. in it—and sat on a cot for the next two hours waiting for the alert to be over (it turned out to be a practice). I was late for curfew because the alert wasn't over which was fun, especially since I had been illegally late two nights before and I had had my curfew cut down to 11:00. Fun times in Vietnam!

Letter. July 23, An Khe

Alert just sounded…. Just a practice—only lasted 15 minutes. I was outside after it was over, yelling to the guys going back to their barracks after they'd gone to the bunkers (in the pouring rain), yelling "good-night, guys, wasn't that a fun alert," and who should walk up, sopping wet, but the major, the CO of the hospital which is near the Center, scowling to tell us our Center light had been left on again and had to be shot out again! I felt a bit like a fool!

Letter. Oct. 1, Danang

Everyone expected terrible things to happen because of the election [Vietnamese national election for president] and we were given extra Marine guards to supplement our feeble little gook guards. We were restricted to our billet for Saturday night to Monday morning.

We were all prepared to be totally bored but actually it turned out to be quite fun. All sorts of nice people brought us food, and a guy I've been dating brought us steaks so we had a steak fry. It was strictly illegal for him to come and he probably could have gotten court-marshalled if he'd been caught.

Saturday and Sunday night we had to all sleep downstairs in

two rooms which was rather cozy. This was so that we could get out of our house fast if we had to. Nothing happened the first night—no one was really too nervous but it was pretty exciting. Then the next night when we were all sleeping, a shot hit our house which had been fired by a sniper. We all hit the deck and stayed there for a while until more Marines came and then the situation was well in hand so we went back to sleep.

Letter. Dec., Cu Chi

About two nights after I was here we had a mortar attack—my first one. Since then we've had one more real one and three more alerts. Nothing bad ever happens. Some mortars come in and nothing happens. Two of them in the same night in fact. One of them was just an alert and the other was the real thing.

I had this really horrible dream when I was in Japan on R&R. I've only had two nightmares about the war since I've been here. This one was that the base camp of Cu Chi got overrun. When I got back here I told a guy my dream and then that same night they tried to overrun a camp about six miles just outside of Cu Chi. They didn't overrun it, but they tried. He said from now on, if I ever have a dream be sure and tell him because he has faith in my dreams now.

Tape. Jan. 12, Cu Chi

One night before Christmas they told us that we were to sit in bunkers because they were expecting an alert. They told us to go in about quarter to 7 until quarter past 7.

It was really dumb. We had incoming rounds not too long ago. It happens, but they haven't been as recent as when I first got here. It keeps it exciting. I can sleep through the most amazing noises now. Sometimes the artillery is really loud going out, but I can sleep through anything. It is really fantastic. On quiet nights it seems strange.

Emily Strange was our unofficial and much-loved poet laureate. She loved reunions and gatherings at the Wall, coming to all our Donut Dollie reunions and also those of the Mobile Riverine Force and

9th Infantry Division where she spent nine months of her tour. She was invited numerous times to their reunions to give her funny and touching speeches. Emily died in July 2016, brave and laughing until the end, especially when she got her bucket list wish to fly in a glider two weeks before her death. She wrote this song about alerts with Barbara Hager, Special Services, and many poems.

Incoming

(Chorus)
Incoming, Incoming,
Can't you hear those sirens, don't you see those flares,
Ol' Charlie's playing games again.
Incoming, Incoming,
Grab your poncho liner and cigarettes and bring a friend.

(Verse 1)
I applied for Vietnam, a weak moment understand.
Came over here to build morale in this never - never land.
They briefed us on the monsoon rains and the Mekong Delta dust,
But they didn't mention one damn word about the mortars fired at us.

(Chorus)

(Verse 2)
Standing in the shower stall, the water's trickling slow.
The dogs are staring at your bod and the bugs put on a show.
You're all soaped up and getting clean, you're scrubbing down your back,
Then the siren blasts, the MP yells, it's another damned attack.

(Chorus)

(Verse 3)
To be awakened in the dark of night is really quite a strain.
Those funny sounds like thunder from an early morning rain.
The sudden realization and both feet hit the floor.
I'm headin' up and I'm movin' out, but I can't unlock the door.

(Chorus)

Emily Strange, Donut Dollie and
Barbara Hager, Army Special Services
in Dong Tam, Vietnam
©1969

Here's Emily playing her guitar with guys in the Delta

Donut Dollies

6

Our official Red Cross uniforms were formless seersucker baby-blue dresses that were comfortable but totally impractical, or culottes that were only slightly more practical and perhaps even more unflattering. The good part about them is that we were easily recognizable as being totally out of place.

This is a story about General John Tolson and our uniforms. General Tolson and I came in country at the same time, April '67, and he was the 1st Cav commander until July '69. He was a great supporter of the Red Cross girls, encouraging his people to get us out to the forward units as much as possible.

Letter. June 23, An Khe

Today I went to the field to assist at a change of command ceremony. The general who came to do the honors had to rush off right away because two companies had just made contact and he had to get back to direct. He's a really cool general, Tolson. He treats us like we belong to him and always makes a special point of coming over and talking to us if he sees us in the field, introducing us as "his girls."

I remember his comment on that day, something to the effect that, "Isn't it something that here we are in flak jacket, helmets, weapons, etc., and there those girls are in their blue dresses." He said it with admiration, that we should risk being there unprotected just so we could be with the troops.

Sharon (Vander Ven) Cummings tells her own story about the appreciation generals had for us and our incongruous presence in the field.

One day, after completing our programming at Dau Tieng, one of the generals stopped in his helicopter and told us to get in, which of course we did. He had some troops digging in somewhere and decided we should go down and see them. So there we were, in "war zone C," in our powder blue uniforms, smiling and being our cheerful selves while the guys were in camouflage and digging in for a battle. Both the guys and we wondered what we were doing there that day!

Suzi Baiamonte Conklin has her own baby-blue dress story when she was at Lai Khe, the home of the Big Red One (1st Infantry Division), in July, 1968.

The day started with my partner Linda (Sullivan Schulte) and I on the Lai Khe airstrip trying to make our weekly run near Quan Loi. We were in competition with a news team looking for helicopters "to get to the action," so we grabbed the first available chopper. Once at Quan Loi, our usual Huey to our destination, a remote airstrip near the Cambodian border, was not available so we were put on a Chinook. Noise is a factor in riding a Chinook, making it hard to hear. The pilot wrote down a message asking if we were sure we wanted to go to this airstrip. "Of course," we wrote back. We could see the airstrip, but the pilot landed (more like hovered) a short distance from it, letting us off quickly and throwing down our program bag.

As we walked to the airstrip, I realized there were no GIs, only Vietnamese civilians who were quite far away. In a quandary, we opened the prop bag to program with them. In retrospect, I will say that they were just as puzzled as we were. Overhead, I heard a Huey that landed a couple hundred yards from us. I saw a GI running towards us. "What are you doing here," he asked, and I replied, "Programming, do you want to play?" In answer, he started throwing the props back into the bag. He grabbed me by one arm and I had Linda by the other as we did a fast trot to the Huey.

Apparently, the general in the chopper had seen "two blue dots" on the airstrip and realized the dots were Donut Dollies in the wrong place at a very wrong time. General Talbott got a medal for saving us and I got a story.

During the Persian Gulf War I became acquainted with a woman in Washington, DC, who was involved with Vietnam veteran activities and organizations. She very much wanted to participate in Desert Storm and going as a Red Cross DD or its equivalent if it existed was what she wanted. She applied but it didn't work out. During this time, she acquired a Red Cross dress, the blue seersucker ones we wore.

At the next Memorial Day or Veterans Day I saw her at the Wall wearing the dress. I asked about it and she said she'd been made an honorary Donut Dollie. I can't speak to the circumstances of that because I didn't ask.

What I do remember is a flash of disbelief and anger, and my response that she hadn't earned it. I could have added that she hadn't spent the year in Vietnam, gotten it dirty with the red dust or black pentaprime and sweat, hadn't tried to maintain her dignity and modesty while hopping on and off choppers and jeeps without showing all, hadn't felt stupid standing on a firebase in a blue dress surrounded by men fully armed ready for battle, hadn't spent years looking at that dress with its Cav patch on the shoulder hanging in her closet and felt the longing to put it on again to be with the men, and hadn't rejoiced in having that opportunity once again when the Wall was built and we finally came together again.

She didn't deserve to hear the vet who rode by on the Run for the Wall call out, "Hey Donut Dollie," to have a guy hand her a cloth heart because he was giving one to all the women who served, to get a kiss on the cheek from a vet who said he always wanted to kiss a Donut Dollie.

All she had done was put on a dress.

We Donut Dollies were given various nicknames by the men, just as they gave each other nicknames—for instance, Chopper Chicks and Kool-Aid Kids. I once heard that chopper pilots referred to a couple of girls after a long hard day at a firebase as Crumbling Cookies. We were proud of our nickname as it was understood by the men in Vietnam, but now in civilian life in this day and age, it can be a source of "confusion," to say the least.

In this email I tell about how there were others who didn't appreciate our nickname either.

After I came back from Vietnam, I went to visit a DD I'd been stationed with at An Khe who had returned to work for National Red Cross in Washington, DC. I had lunch with my DD friend and our Washington supervisor who was a stickler for using the correct term for our program—SRAO, Supplemental Recreation Activities Overseas. And she hated the term "Donut Dollie," I think because she thought it was demeaning and didn't understand that it was an affectionate nickname for us. In any case, I slipped and said something about Donut Dollies. She was quick to tell me, "You weren't Donut Dollies." I was stunned because I couldn't figure out what else to call us, and so was rendered speechless.

While there, I was asked to speak to the incoming group of girls who were on their way to Vietnam. The only part I remember is that I said that I was fortunate to have been assigned to three combat units. It was pointed out to me that I shouldn't have said that because lots of girls would be going to support units. Oh well....

In many ways, we Donut Dollies were fish out of water, both while in Vietnam and back in the States. We were civilian, not military; we were women, not men; we were volunteers, not draftees; our job was to interact with the enlisted men, not officers.

I've just been reading messages on an email group about officers and EMs and the need to salute and how they resented it. One of the things I really liked about being a DD is that our honchos came from the ranks and I never felt "lorded over" (although I must admit that at times we did try to get around the rules).

We always brought everyone a little gift when we came back from R&R, and we made Sayonara books for each other when we left a unit in which we highlighted memorable incidents in that girl's tour. I got my Sayonara book from An Khe and Danang, but when I left Cu Chi in April '68, things were kind of disorganized due to Tet, moving our quarters, and life. They promised me one later, and I'm still waiting…. One of my most treasured mementos is the slice of a rotor blade I got as a Sayonara gift from An Khe in August '67. And the piece of the ammo box with a large shard of Tet shrapnel from Cu Chi.

I went to see *Good Morning, Vietnam* with a DD friend and a civilian friend of hers. During the scene where the actor playing Adrian Cronauer was caught in a traffic jam and started kidding with the guys in a nearby truck—where are you from, how long you been in Vietnam, etc.—the whole atmosphere changed from growing frustration to one of lightness and laughter. I whispered to my friend, "He was a Donut Dollie, too."

Then when we came out of the movie, after the ending in which Louis Armstrong sang "What a wonderful world" to scenes of destruction in Vietnam, I said to her, "I feel like bawling." She responded something like, "That was so depressing." The civilian woman said, "What? I thought it was funny!"

My DD friend in DC and I went to a talk by Morley Safer who had just written a book about going back to Vietnam called *Flashbacks*. Afterwards she bought the book and we waited in line for him to autograph it. As he was signing it, I asked if he had ever seen any Donut Dollies when he was reporting in Vietnam. After a pause, while I assume it sunk in, he lifted his head up and asked, "Were you two Donut Dollies?" When we said yes, he said, "No, I never saw any of you because you were always too far forward." We just beamed!!!

This is an email to the Donut Dollie email group which I knew they, but perhaps not others, would understand.

I had a fun experience tonight. I was out with some friends at a watering hole here in Fairbanks where I noticed a table of about 10 GIs who looked different than the usual ones we might see there. First, they were older—mid-30s or so, no women, lots of guys and yet a quiet group. After about an hour of another woman and I goading each other on (I can't believe it took me so long), finally I went over to ask what their story was. Turns out they were an infantry group (we thought they were flyers) from Hawaii doing some kind of training for two weeks in the Alaskan bush.

But what was so neat was just chatting with them for a few minutes—one guy trying to tell me they were there on a secret missile mission as the others grinned, joking about how this was cold weather ops for them, where was their tan if they were from Hawaii—you know the patter. It was a brief nostalgic moment of being a Donut Dollie in Vietnam.

Once a Donut Dollie, always a Donut Dollie!

Hooches

7

I think my favorite of our living quarters was at An Khe in '67. As I described it in a letter: "The billets are much better than expected (wooden, showers, flush toilets, etc.)." The building was a square with a grassy area in the middle. The DDs were on one side, the nurses on the other; bathroom at one end and a day room with TV (which I never remember watching) at the other.

Our billet at Cu Chi was much the same in that we had two buildings with grassy area and a bunker in the middle, surrounded by a fence. It was right next to headquarters which was blown up (along with my departure certificate) during Tet. We spent a lot of time in the above-ground bunker during Tet for which we Donut Dollies had filled sand bags to reinforce it. They then built us a one-building dormitory-like hooch with a hall running between all the rooms and an underground bunker outside the building.

In Danang we lived in a two-story "villa" with a yard near the Officers' Mess where we ate. The roof leaked, so we had to move our beds around when it rained. We would take cover in the bathroom when we were being shot at as we waited for the Marines to come and take over from the White Mice (Vietnamese policemen) who "guarded" us. Vietnamese women (mama-sans) cleaned the hooch and did our laundry. One was an old mama-san who told me (in sign language) not to leave my money lying around or the other hooch maids would steal it.

Tape. Dec., Cu Chi

We live in these hooches which are substandard even by army standards, and they won't improve them. Once we had a great horde of bugs, huge bugs, in our office which were absolutely terrible— all over the ceiling and the floor and everything. Then we sprayed it all and they all fell down all over the floor and everything, but we got rid of them. Since it is substandard they won't put in screens to keep the bugs out. It's really swampy here too. They're building us a new hooch and we should be moving into that in about a month.

Sunbathing in front of our first bunker at Cu Chi

Tape. Feb. 28, Cu Chi

They are building us a new hooch, a great big huge thing and the bunker is actually fantastic. It's underground and it's going to have something like eight feet of cement on top. They have made practically a house underground. I don't know when they're going to get it finished, but it is really going to be beautiful. And I think I'll have to end up sleeping there just about every night because I'm getting short, you see. 57 days to go.

Sharon (Vander Ven) Cummings describes living conditions in two of her assignments.

In November I was transferred from Cam Ranh to the center at II Field Forces, Long Binh. The girls stationed here all lived in Bien Hoa, at the Honor Smith Compound, Conley 10-A, affectionately known as the Pink Palace. This French villa even had a flush toilet and a bathtub! Definitely different than Cam Ranh where we had an outhouse (called the "Rose Room") and "showers" hooked up to huge water drums on the roof!"

Playing Games

8

Our "job" is hard to explain and even harder to understand. In this email to the veteran group, some of whom had seen us in Vietnam, others who had only heard about us and still others who really didn't have a clue, I give it a shot.

Red Cross Recreation Workers, a.k.a., Donut Dollies, played games. It was our mission, our job, what we were sent to Vietnam to do. We played games in mess halls, on flight lines, in recreation centers, on LZ's, firebases, along the road—wherever there were GIs. The games were usually a cross between a TV quiz show and a board game. We made them up with themes like sports, cars, the States, travel—and best of all, women. We'd gather the guys together, divide them into teams, and then pit them against each other, asking the teams questions as they tried to advance from point A to Z.

Some of my favorite stories. (You have to suspend your disbelief when you read these. It really is unbelievable that we could get these hardened warriors to do these things, but then, we did have round-eyes!) For one game we used children's alphabet blocks with which the men spelled out the answer by standing in line holding a block. My favorite part was at the end when I would say, "Do you guys realize that you've just spent the last hour playing with kiddies' blocks?" The moans could be heard for miles (oops, klicks).

In another game we had a board in front and gave the teams the answers on cards that they were supposed to run up and hang on the nails on the board. One guy got so enthusiastic that he impaled himself on the nail, but happily went right on playing.

Another time, a guy fell and hurt his knee so badly in the run that he had to go to the infirmary.

My favorite game was based on Concentration. We cut out the faces of the Playmates of the Month, put them on a big board covered over, then had teams try to match the pairs of faces. The reaction when the first card was turned over and they realized what they were seeing was great. We girls eventually learned which month each of the playmates was from. The best part was the "wildcard." Do you remember the picture of the grizzly old man with no teeth? Well, he was behind one of the cards and when the guys saw him, the hoots that greeted the playmates was nothing compared to what he got!

This game-playing took place wherever we could gather a crowd. However, at firebases it wasn't always possible or advisable to get a group together, so we didn't use our "organized" games. Our time there was spent visiting in bunkers, artillery gun pits, serving in the chow lines, wherever there were GIs.

If the opportunity arose we had an informal program—our "bag of tricks." This consisted of string, rubber bands, flashcards, just ourselves, with which we could amaze and mystify the men. This impromptu program, which we called "Women are superior to men," consisted of a variety of feats of strength, coordination, and mental abilities (read "telepathy") which demonstrated unequivocally the superiority of women.

For example, a demonstration of women's superior coordination. Kneel on the ground, put your elbow against your knee and stretch your arm out straight on the ground. Put a cigarette pack at the end of your fingertips, hold your hands behind your back, and then try to knock over the pack with your nose. We ladies can do this with ease. Guys, on the other hand, will fall on their faces because men's weight is in their upper bodies and women's is elsewhere.

I had some favorite groups that I went to as frequently as possible. One was the Radio Research Unit at Cu Chi. They were helpful in correcting us when the answers we'd made up were wrong. Another was the LRRPs of the 25th Infantry Division who had great team spirit. They were a really rambunctious, friendly group who loved our games (or us!). We hardly had to do anything other than present the game because they entered into it with such enthusiasm, egging each other on, harassing, tricking, criticizing, and generally raising Cain with each other. However, one day they were totally unresponsive. We just couldn't get them interested in any part of the game. It was about "Famous People," so finally, in order to get their interest, I asked, "Who's the most famous person in your unit?" There was a pause, then a name. I said, "I don't remember him, is he here?" They said, no, he'd been killed a few days earlier. The game was over. We sat and talked with them until it was time to leave.

The war was never far away. I remember being on an LZ with the 1st Cav where we were playing games and talking to the guys while they waited to be airlifted out to the bush.

Nancy on an LZ surrounded by men preparing to be airlifted out

Within an hour of their departure, before we had left the LZ, we received word that they had made contact and several had been killed. Another time we were doing a quick informal program with a unit before they went out on a convoy from an LZ. The CO interrupted us, saying it was time to saddle up. As we were still gathering our game together, we heard him telling them that if a vehicle hit a mine to go on around it and keep on going because it might be an ambush, that someone else would be along to pick them up. The transition between playing games with Donut Dollies in blue dresses to a possible ambush was sur-real.

We also visited in hospitals regularly. Whenever we went into a ward, we wouldn't leave until we had talked individually with every man in there. We quickly learned that it was easier to talk with them if we looked only at their eyes and nowhere else. The opening questions were usually the same—what unit are you with, where are you from—but this was enough to start a conversation which could lead away from their wounds and the war. Visiting in hospitals was hard, real hard, but also the most rewarding.

But the best times of all were when we weren't "on," when we could just stop at an LZ or in the hospital or at a stand down or eating a meal and talk to one or two lonely guys, and believe that we had, in fact, made a difference.

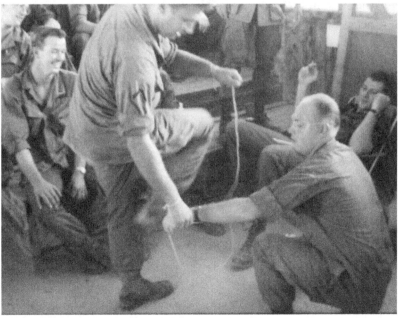

Playing string game with the LRRPs at Cu Chi

J. Holley (McAleese) Watts wrote a little book of poems titled "Who Knew? Reflections on Vietnam," which I can't read more than a page or two at a time because the waves of nostalgia that her few words evoke overwhelm me.

WHO KNEW...

just how bad it had been for them the day before.
We flew out to see the unit with our "TV Theme Songs"
program,
usually a winner, but not here.
Even the gunny was disheartened.

He stood there silently watching us hold up each TV show
name card,
a dark look gripping his black face.

The men competed half-heartedly to sing (or yell out) the
theme songs
occasionally glancing his way yet still he seemed unmoved.

Then I held up "Mickey Mouse Club"
And he stepped forward suddenly, his fist punching out
M-I-C See ya real soon!
K-E-Y...

Everyone cheered.
I don't think there was a dry eye in the place.

J. Holley (McAleese) Watts

This poem by Emily Strange offers another perspective of the effect our work could have.

JOB DESCRIPTION:
DONUT DOLLIE

i flew to desolate fire bases
filled with the tools of war
and the men who used them

it was my job to perform the miracle
of making the war disappear
(however briefly)
for boys who had been trained to kill

it was my mission to raise the morale
of children who had grown old too soon
watching friends die

it was my calling
to take away fear and replace it with hope
to return sanity to a world gone insane

i was the mistress of illusion
as i pulled smiles from the dust and heat
the magical genie of "back-in-the-world"
as i created laughter in the mud

but when the show was over
i crawled back into my bottle
and pulled the cork in tightly behind me

©1992

Programming

9

The Red Cross called it Clubmobiling, but the word we used to identify our work was "programming." This referred to the games we made up that could be done "formally" in recreation centers or informally at base camps or in the field by traveling to LZs and firebases. However, there were many other ways of interacting with the men, many occurring spontaneously as opportunities presented themselves.

In the Recreation Centers

I was very fortunate to be stationed first with the Cav (recreation center and beaucoup runs), then Danang (center and few runs), and then Cu Chi (no center). I really really missed not having a center there. It was great to be able to make friends that you could get to know because they came to the center regularly. That was less easy in Danang because the Marines were mostly passing through, but there were still more chances to hang rather than just be on a FB or LZ briefly.

My first day in the rec center at An Khe I peeked out the office door into the center at a sea of OD green and men! I ducked back in and said in panic to the UD, "What do I do??" She said, "Follow me," took me to a table of guys, asked if we could join them (sure thing!), asked them one of our really original opening questions like, where are you from or how long have you been here or what's your unit (rocket science, huh?), waited for the response, and then got up and LEFT ME! I was on my own from then on out.

I refer to it as my OJT.

Letter. June 23, An Khe

At the Center we serve coffee and Kool-Aid all the time and sometimes cookies when we have them. During the day we don't have a program there, but there are always games for the guys to play and cards galore. At night we have some sort of a program, like the Italian night or a Sadie Hawkins night which I just did.

It was a real blast where I proved the superiority of women in various ways and gave the guys a wolf test to find out how lecherous they are. After I told them to guess what a girl carries in her handbag, I emptied mine for them. There were things in it like ear plugs, dog tags, can opener and a bottle opener plus hundreds of other things which I always carry around. They couldn't believe it!!

Letter. May 29, An Khe

I've had a clubmobile program due and two center programs two nights in a row. Last night was Italian night, and we had pizza and played a tic-tac-toe game with questions about Italy. I was MC and turned into a real ham. It's very easy to do when you're in front of 150 guys with a microphone in your hand. I was hardly nervous at all—just a ham. It was a fun but traumatic evening because the pizza came 1½ hours late. Tonight I'm in charge of the photo contest, which is a real farce because there are only about 20 entries. I really dread it.

Note to me from another girl after the Italian night.

To mai fren Nanci,

Wal kiddo, yu hada biga sucesa lasta nighta. Mama dint tink data a yunga bootifulls senorita lika you coulda hava so mucha talent, two.

I mustamit data da pizza was a bono idee, joost goze to sho data kid frum new Jurzee kana doo it. Done eva letaneeone sa nuten bad abowt yu stayt... Nanci mai fren, yu showeda alla dose smartamouths lasta ngihta. Nowa day see data smarta folksa cumma from Jurzee two.

Remember data we alla luva yu, anda ara prowda yu; anada we won ever say anyting more badabowt yor state. An ifa yu a guda keeda Mama mite letta yu doo more an more an more an more an more an more an …… more stuffa inda Senter. HOKAY Kiddo???

> Lasagna an ravioli to yu,
> Mama

I had some great dresses over there, some of which my mother sent to me. There were a couple of tent dresses with very bright colors, and a chemise dress with a zipper…that worked…from the neck to the hem line with a large ring at the top of the zipper that I clutched when I was feeling insecure in my surroundings. And best of all was a paper dress! We had a fashion show at the An Khe rec center, and when I paraded around with that paper dress, it was amazing how quickly those zippos came out!

Letter. June 29, An Khe

We also have nights when a band comes and plays, but we don't dance. That would be disastrous. Also, volleyball, ping pong, pinochle tournaments, etc., etc., ad infinitum. During the day we just generally talk to the guys and try to circulate as much as possible. That is our only chance to talk to them for any length of time and get to know individual guys. I think that is the most satisfying part of the job, although going to the field is great too. When we go to the field we just talk to the guys as they work.

Letter. Oct. 1, Danang

One really cool time I had here with the EMs was a day in the Danang center when one of my special people was there—a really cute little friendly guy, and he was kind of nutty and funny. We ended up playing spoons and card games on the dirty old floor in the middle of the center. There were about five of us playing and everyone else thought we were nuts—almost as bad as the time we played jump rope and hopscotch with the big tough Marines in the center!

In the Field

Nancy Caracciolo Warner's assignments in 1969-70 were first at Lai Khe with the 1st Infantry Division, then An Khe when the 4th ID was there, and finally Danang. This is her response on a questionnaire from a student asking, "What were the average days like?"

Generally we were up early in the morning. We had to catch rides to our destinations. Often those rides were prearranged, but sometimes we would be out on the flight line, or in the motor pool, begging rides to get where we needed to go. Days were long since, as much as we preplanned the day, things were unpredictable. We were always negotiating for everything. First it would be for transportation, then it would be with first sergeants or CO's to ask for permission to gather the men together, then it would be with the men to see if we could inspire them to participate in the game we had brought along. The goal was to have them involved in something so silly that they would, for however briefly, forget about the war. It also was a vehicle that allowed two women to "talk" to 120 guys in one hour!

Conditions were quite variable. It might be hot and we would have to program out in the blazing sun. It might be monsoon season and we would be undercover but having to traverse muddy firebases or base camps in our sneakers while being pelted with torrential downpours.

If you were in the center all day, you had not one moment to yourself to even think. Guys were in and out all day and wanted to talk to you, play cards with you, play pool with you, just be somehow engaged with an American girl in whatever way they could be. Then, once finally home, showered and fed, we would have to attend a party somewhere that would often take us until our curfew—midnight.

Letter. May 2, An Khe

We go forward into the field about once a week in helicopters—too bad not more. And we take a program around to the various units on this base twice a week. Tomorrow's my first time—panic!

[Next day]. Yesterday I went out to the field for the first time and had three helicopter rides—two on small 8-seater Huey's and one on a troop-transport chopper called a Chinook. It was so great!! On the first ride, the pilots knew it was my first ride so we went really low, skimming over tree tops and zig-zagging around, buzzing little Vietnamese farmers. I heard later they were trying to scare me, but I love it! The land here is really pretty—green mountains, well-organized rice paddies, etc. In the field we went to three LZ's and just talked to the guys as they worked and then we ate. It was really pretty fun—very tiring, but exciting.

At An Khe in our preferred transportation to LZs and firebases

Years later I visited on the set of the TV show *China Beach*. They were shooting an episode when new Donut Dollies were flying to their first unit. The actresses asked me if they should

be afraid. I emphatically said no, we were excited, and so they changed the way they had planned to portray their first flight.

Letter. May 11, An Khe

Staff is down to six instead of nine. Yesterday I went to the field again—didn't get a chopper ride unfortunately but got two rides on tanks—they're really a gas. It's great to see the guys in the field because they're so pleased and surprised to see us, and it means a lot to them. You wouldn't believe how dirty I was when I got back—20 miles along dusty road in a completely open jeep and then rain, so it all turned to mud on me. But it's worth it. I really wonder how I'm going to last a year though.

Letter. July 23, An Khe

An LZ is a landing zone, i.e., a base in the field out of base camp (An Khe) where the forward headquarters of the unit operating in that area are. It's like a smaller base camp with chopper and headquarters areas. Smaller LZs or firebases are set up and operated out of by one or two infantry units and have "permanent" artillery units. These LZs are closed as the enemy moves on or an operation is finished. Those are the ones we try to get out to most, to see the infantry who come in for a few day rest from operations.

We go out to them in choppers which are the most wonderful vehicle ever. When they leave the doors open (usually), it's almost like flying free. It's really beautiful!

At LZs we usually just talk to the guys in the bunkers or at work and sometimes we program. At base camp and the big LZs, we have regular stops at the units every week where we program. Programs are mostly about anything—the most recent about weather, comic strips, the one I did about Italy, the States, baseball, the Wild West, etc. We have warm-up games like cards with pictures and they guess what cartoon character it represents (a doghouse for Snoopy), or baseball player (a baby for Babe Ruth), or mixed up words like "temperature" in scrambled order, which they unscramble and yell out the answer. Then there's a main game—

answer questions about baseball to get players around the bases on the boards we make, or about whether to fly home via Okinawa, Philippines, or the Wild West with a ranch or saddle, and whoever answers the question first gets it. There's always a main game on a big board.

Donut Dollies programming with the Big Red One
(1st Infantry Division) in III Corps

Letter. Oct. 1, Danang

The next big exciting thing that happened was a 5-day TDY assignment to Chu Lai, a place about 30 miles south of Danang. I really had a good time and needed to go because at that point I was getting upset with Danang, and it was beautiful to go to a place where we went out into the field again. I have become very stagnant and unenthusiastic. Anyway, at Chu Lai we went into the field and talked to the guys almost like we did in the Cav, but of course it wasn't as great because it wasn't my guys. One of the most fun things I did while I was there was at a cook-out that we were invited to.

There were some EMs sort of in the background who had been invited but felt out of place. They were sitting around playing buzz, so when I got bored with all the brass (which didn't take long), I went over to talk to them and we sat around and played buzz and drank beer (whenever you missed) for about two hours. It was really fun and we hardly ever get to do things like that here because we never see them after hours.

Tape. Nov., Danang

The other day a couple of us were at one of our stops which is always great fun. The guys harass us and really give us a hard time. They accuse us of cheating and they shout so you can hardly talk over the noise they make. We were flipping a coin to see which team would go first, and when Cindy flipped the coin, it went down her dress. The guys nearly died laughing and, of course, we did too. Cindy said it was the most embarrassing thing that had ever happened to her.

In response to overwhelming requests (well, two) from you guys for information about women's toilets, here goes! 1) There weren't any (except at our hooches), and 2) I don't remember ever having to go at a firebase. I have a good constitution and planned it very carefully by having almost nothing to drink while away from base camp. I'm surprised I didn't dehydrate and get medevaced.

Sometimes the guys built us latrines if we went to a firebase or LZ regularly. I understand there were pink ones, flowered ones, wall-papered ones, but I don't remember actually seeing any.

What I do remember is being told by the more seasoned Donut Dollies that it really wasn't a good idea to wave at guys as we went by in the jeep (we waved at everybody, all the time, without fail) if they were standing in an open space with their hands in front of their middle.

René Johnson, who was stationed in 1969-70 at Chu Lai with the Americal Division and later at Cu Chi with the 25th Inf. Div., describes one toilet that was very special.

DDs' outhouse at
Nui Ba Den

My Favorite Gift

Our job was fun, rewarding, exciting – all that we could hope for. But there were sometimes "difficulties," the most prevalent one being access to certain "facilities" during our long days out in the field.

When I was with the 25th Infantry Division at Cu Chi, one of our favorite places to visit was the top of Nui Ba Den where the main operation was a radio relay unit. With the small unit of only about 150 men at the top of the mountain and the 25th providing security at the bottom, the saying was, "We own the top and we own the bottom. The VC own everything in between." The mountain was riddled with tunnels used by the Viet Cong who would come out at night and lob mortars at the top and at the units below.

Our entire unit was going to be visiting a number of bases with a special Christmas program, so the commanding officer asked if we could come up to Nui Ba Den for our first stop on Christmas morning to help pass out the presents they had received from people in the States. Of course we could!! Early on Christmas morning, we flew to the top of the mountain, had breakfast with the men, and then, when it when the gift-giving time arrived, we found that we were actually there to receive a gift: our very own pink, one-hole, enclosed-for-privacy "Far Out House"!!

Emily Strange writes about the ambivalent feelings we and the men had about our visits to the forward areas.

Men Digging In

another firebase playing silly games;
anything to help them remember that
the "Real World" still existed and that
their families were still waiting to
welcome them home

some greeted us at the chopper,
carried our game bag,
obviously thrilled to see
a round eye in a skirt
(these eagerly participated in
our silly games)
others came shyly late,
not sure they would know
how to act around girl women
after being in the bush

for far too long;
but, if they stayed,
the eager ones usually
teased them into participating
and even these reticent ones seemed
to transcend the war
(if only momentarily)
as they tried to be the first
to yell out that
Country Joe and the Fish
recorded
"I'm Fixin'-To-Die-Rag"

still, i often wondered if
i was just bringing them lies;
feared they would never again see
the "Real World"
and that their families would not
welcome home their coffins

some never came at all
too macho
or too afraid to remember
that there was another world

maybe they were right;
was i really doing anything
that would change the reality of war
or any outcome for the men who fought it?

———————————

down the road there were some men
who'd been in heavy contact, taken casualties,
scared, angry, sad, confused, depressed;
would my partner and i go see them?

(truthfully, i would go anywhere
i was allowed to go
and some places i probably
wouldn't have been allowed
had i bothered to ask)

two jeeps appeared
50 cal machine gun
mounted
on the front of one

men wearing flak jackets
steel pots
carrying varying weapons
and two donut dollies
(their light blue uniforms
making excellent targets)
drove silently down the road
for what seemed a long time
in this land of sudden death,
then pulled off the dirt path
and came to a halt

i could see maybe 15 boy men
digging in for the night
wearing tattered uniforms
and thousand yard stares
which were unchanged
by the arrival of our jeeps

i got out and began
walking toward them
as they continued to dig,
oblivious to my presence
until i stood closely
in front of one boy

as he looked up
his thousand yard stare
momentarily looked past me,
through me,
then transformed to confusion
becoming bewilderment

(a donut dollie was the
last thing he had expected
to see)

thereupon his eyes revealed a realization:
"if the donut dollies are here,
i must be safe"
(the absurdity of that
assumption escaped us both)
and a twinkle appeared in his eyes
which rippled across his face
producing the smile of a
child receiving his first puppy

we exchanged pleasantries,
talked of nothing
in particular nor memorable;
yet, it was a conversation
as intimate and healing
as a baptism of the born again

the others continued digging,
survival being the object of this game
whose score was tallied in body counts
(they had too recently added
the bodies of their own)

so i walked among the deepening holes
and spoke to each digger;

comforting, encouraging, laughing, joking,
pretending that the war would not reach
this tiny piece of earth

for i finally understood
that even if these holes were to
ultimately be their own graves
from which God
chose to reclaim their souls,
at least He had allowed me to help Him
grant their last wish:
to once again remember those in the
"Real World" waiting to welcome them home,
and to feel safe in the remembering

———————————

on that day, i knew
that it did not matter
whether i had brought
lies or truths;
it mattered only that
i had come

©1992

Other Duties as Assigned (or not)

We had daily schedules that determined whether we would be in the rec center, go on a programing run around the base or to the forward bases or have an occasional office day. Sometimes our schedules included evening activities as well.

On our one day off a week, we were free to do whatever we wanted which could be washing clothes, visiting friends, sleeping, going into town, etc. However, no day or evening was ever completely predictable.

Letter. May 11, An Khe

Today is my day off. This morning I went down to the dispensary in town run by the US to distribute some clothes sent from home to the kids here. It was a harrowing experience, not so much because of the poverty, but because there were so many hands reaching out and small faces, and it was impossible to tell who you had given something. The kids here are absolutely darling—among the cutest I've ever see. We went into the "maternity ward," such as it was. The women were using newspaper for diapers. We passed out boxes of Kotex to them—it makes me laugh to think about the various ways they're going to be used.

Letter. Oct. 1, Danang

A Navy dentist I'm dating took me on a MedCap he does about every other week when he goes to this Buddhist temple and performs dentistry on anybody who wants it. All he can do there is pull teeth because there's no equipment.

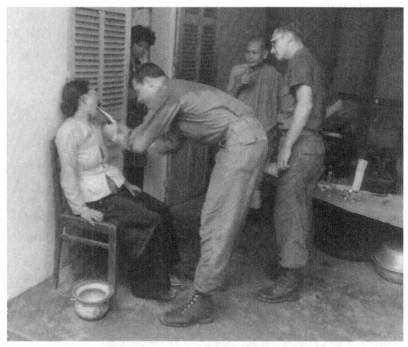

Barry, the dentist, pulling teeth on a Medcap near Danang

It was very interesting and fun to see the Vietnamese people like this because I really don't like them because of all the stories guys tell about their experiences in the field. But this makes me realize that they're people after all and need help and some are good and some are bad.

Tape. Cu Chi

Today was really great because we went to a place where, although it's near here, the guys never see girls. So we did our program and then sat down on the ground and drew pictures and doodles in the sand for half an hour. Mucho fun and informal, just like playing cards on the floor at the center.

Tape. Dec. 22, Cu Chi

A brigade of the 101st Airborne came through Cu Chi from the States. We waited for three hours with balloons and signs and candy canes and other stuff to give them, and of course Kool-Aid. All these guys, brand new from the States, with brand new flak jackets and canteens and the whole business. They were acting all tough because they're Airborne, and Airborne is the greatest, you know, but one of the sergeants told me these guys were really scared. A lot of them were wearing other patches because somebody told me 50% of them are back for their second tour. I talked to about five who had been in infantry units in the Cav.

I wore the Screaming Eagle patch hung over my nametag while with them. That evening as I was walking to our chow hall, I got some sour looks from the 25th Infantry guys and couldn't figure out why until I realized I still had the 101st patch on.

When we were with a unit, we were THEIRS!!

Tape. Jan. 1, Cu Chi

I don't think I told you about what we did Christmas. We had been told we were going to be able to get out in the field and see guys, see lots of infantry in the field. Then at the last minute the stupid G-1 [Personnel Officer] who's been in charge of letting us go out in the field said we couldn't go. And so what we did finally was just go out to this really secure little place where we saw maybe fifty guys at the most—I think they were artillery—and we passed out the presents. Then after we got back here, another girl named Nancy who I really have fun with and I went to all our favorite places. We went to Radio Research, what we call R&R for short. Then we went over to the 101st and rode on a mule, which is a flat car, and then we went over to the Scout Dogs and talked to them, and then we went to some aviation place and passed out goodie bags. We just ran all afternoon. It didn't seem like Christmas; it just seemed like a holiday. And what was really nice about it was that lots of the guys were let off for the afternoon so it looked like a weekend at home because there were all these guys out in the field playing baseball and throwing a football around. It was beautiful. It just looked so much like home. And you know the guys were happy. It was good.

Tape. Jan. 12, Cu Chi

I have to tell you about the Bob Hope show. I managed to sit in a seat which was absolutely the farthest back so I barely saw him. We had binoculars, but they put up movie cameras on stands so he was standing behind that the whole time, so I really didn't get to see him. The reason I was so far back is because I couldn't find any decent seats up front and there were some guys I knew on dusters (small tanks) in the back, so they told me to come on up and sit on it. It was fun seeing it with those guys. I didn't really miss not being able to see much because we were so far back. What I missed was that I wanted to be up there where all the guys were and see them yell and scream at all the girls, but I got some good pictures of the guys watching Raquel Welch, the big attraction. She was the big attraction, and they were really funny when she came on. Bob Hope was pretty disappointing, strangely enough. His jokes seemed very pat, even though he had some specific jokes that pertained to Cu Chi. Still he wasn't as well received as I would have thought which surprised me. I don't know whether it was the area where I was sitting or what it was. But it was good to see it and it will be fun to see the show when they show it back home.

Guys on a duster
watching Bob Hope
Show at Cu Chi

I've just watched the Bob Hope show from the year I was there, '67. I saw it in Cu Chi and the only part of the show that I remember is Rachel Welch in her skimpy dress. Seeing all those laughing sweet young faces of the men makes me nostalgic and sad. The ending is particularly poignant when he expresses his hope that the war will be over soon.... That was December '67....

Tape. Jan. 12, Cu Chi

The Wolfhounds, this really gung ho infantry unit—I guess it's famous even back in the States—came back in the other day and we went out to greet them. They came in in choppers and then were picked up by truck and taken to their area. We rode in the trucks and then we'd ride back to pick up the next load. When we were going, this one truck started shooting flares and smoke things. I think I told you when this happened once before when my favorite mechanized unit (which means tracks or small tanks) came in and they were shooting off flares and smoke bombs. It was really fantastic. They are so beautiful and the guys get so excited. I shot one off the time before and nearly broke my hand off.

Nancy with tankers in Cu Chi AO

Tape. Jan. 30, Cu Chi

The Wolfhounds, one of the infantry units with all sorts of spirit, have come back in and so every night for the last four nights we have been having dinner with the EMs. It's fun to see these guys when they come in from the field, which is rare, because it's the only chance we get to see them. And I find that when I go over there, I recognize two or three guys from the unit even though we never see them in the field, but I recognize them because I've seen them in the hospital.

One of my favorite units at Cu Chi was ASA (Army Security Agency) or RRU (Radio Research Unit) or R&R as we Donut

Dollies called it. We visited R&R every week as part of our regular runs. We'd bring our silly games, using those guys as guinea pigs because we knew they always knew the answers, and they played along like it wasn't the stupidest thing they'd ever done.

I volunteered to do a Sunday run there on one of my days off (yes, we got one, sometimes), and since it was a day off, I didn't feel constrained to totally obey the Red Cross rules. However, when offered a beer, I was reluctant to drink it out of the beer can since I was in uniform and there were strict rules about that. (I could have taken off my pins as one DD did when confronted with a similar situation, thereby rendering her out of uniform.) Instead I asked that he put the beer in a coke can I'd been drinking from. So as we played our silly game, I sipped from the can, finding it tasted a little odd but thinking that was because it was in a coke can...until one of the guys said in a shocked voice, "You're not drinking out of that are you? I've been putting my cigarette ashes in there." Clara Barton struck back.

My R&R buddies modifying their hooch

I also visited these guys on my days off, just to hang out with them. As I wrote in a letter home, "It is really nice to go over there because I don't have to do anything to entertain them. I hardly even have to talk to them. We all just sit around and they babble. I think they like having me there, but it's not like I'm any great center of attraction which is the way I like it."

I have pictures of them, one wearing a beanie with a tiny rotor blade on top, another of us sandbagging their hooch after one of the many mortar attacks during Tet, one of me climbing the radio tower, and several of the cute blond with the slow southern accent named Dave. I have many fond memories of them—their fun, their kindness, and their smarts.

I was too dumb, naive, out-of-the-loop to know that they did anything other than research radios.....

As I learned much later, the Army Security Agency was a signal intelligence gathering unit that provided security for communications and for electronic countermeasures operations. Some of their personnel had top secret clearance.

We were asked to put on one of our programs at the General's Mess at Cu Chi so they could see what the heck we were doing with their men. Linda and I had the honors, and we did one about the Wild West. They got fairly involved and it went pretty well, but nowhere near as much fun as with the men.

And then there was another General's Mess at Cu Chi during which we received incoming. I was nearly trampled in the rush to exit and was the last one out the door. But I guess, in retrospect, their jobs were more important than mine....

We made regular visits to various units on base, one of which was the telephone operators at the communication Quonset hut at Cu Chi. I got to be buds with one of the guys, but one week when I came back he was no longer there. When I asked the guys where he'd gone, they told me the story.

When they'd get several calls coming through at once, some would have to wait. When one person finally got his call responded to, he complained about how long it took. My friend, the telephone operator, said, "Oh, that's nothing. Sometimes I keep the general waiting several minutes." Turns out it was the general he was talking to.

My DJ Career

During my time at Danang, several of the Donut Dollies DJed a radio show over AFVN. Mine was called "The Happening," taken from the Supremes hit which I used as the theme song. That hour of playing records was probably the most stressful thing I encountered in Vietnam, even worse than Tet at Cu Chi! I literally chain smoked the whole time I was on.

One evening the engineer had rewired things such that I couldn't hear myself talking over the radio or hear the music being played. The engineer was in another room where I could see but not hear him. So we started out:

"Hi, this is Nancy with your spotlight album of the week. (Are we on—I can't hear anything.)"

Frantic head nodding and hand waving from the engineer.

"Uh, this week we're going to be playing (is this thing working—I can't hear)"... more frantic nods and waves... "an album by the Beach Boys (what's going on, why isn't it working?)"

Finally he cuts to a song. His phone rings. It's the general, saying (yelling), "Is that girl drunk? What's she doing? Get her off!!!"

The engineer explains. Things calm down. I finish the show, still unable to hear the songs, sitting in an empty silent room, chain smoking and talking to myself. And that's the last time I DJed!

The Men and Me

10

My feelings about the men were on a roller-coaster—up/down, hot/cold, bored/happy/sad/angry—but always passionate. As reflected in my letters, I'd been there less than two weeks and already I was feeling it. (Notice I was calling them "boys," something that soon changed!)

Letter. May 2, An Khe

I just haven't gotten excited about anything really—partly because at the center there are so many boys staring at you I really feel self-conscious. I talked to a few yesterday—very nice—but it's very disrupting because the nicest one is going back into the field today for a month or more. It must be hard to know the guys because they're always moving in and out again.

Letter. May 11 , An Khe

They're all so much alike and yet each is different. Since they're all younger and because of our positions, they're all like younger brothers. Sometimes I get really sick of talking about the same old thing (home state, time in country, etc.), but most every day you find one guy who has something different or interesting to say, or a new way of saying the same old thing, and it refreshes you for the rest.

It's so hard to be nice to everyone and listen to their troubles, but usually they're nice to us so it's okay. And then every now and then, somebody (usually an officer or a drunk GI) will say it really means a lot to the guys having us there—and everything is rosy again.

Another frustrating thing is that just as you get a friend, somebody you can relax and talk with and don't have to feel like a social worker, he goes back into the field for three months or goes home.

About half the division has less than three months, which is sad for us but great for them.

I've met two guys (two of the nice, special ones) who are in the field now doing dangerous things like beating the bush and one is a tunnel rat, and I'm just waiting for the time when one I know gets killed. It's a strange thing to wait for.

Some mornings at the center I feel like yelling at the first guy who speaks to me, and then I go ahead and smile and say, "Yes, I'm from New Jersey," and "Yes, I've heard of Perth Amboy," etc., etc., ad infinitum. I just don't know if I can be nice for a whole year, and I've only been here twelve days! I think the thing a girl needs here most is a boy to talk to, to whom she can say any old thing she want to. It's okay to do that with girls but not the same. Sometimes I really think I'll never want to see a boy again after this year, but then again…!

Today a boy from Boston asked where Washington State is. I was too stunned to answer, so a boy at the table told him and he said, "Oh, I thought that was Washington, D.C."

Letter. May 17, An Khe

Today one of my special friends left for home. I saw him out at the airport as we went on what we call "courtesy calls" where we give cookies and Kool-aid to various people who help us (telephone operators, supply men, etc.). He was waiting for his plane home, and I was just lucky to see him because he's leaving a day early. Another one leaves in seven days. They come back in from the field for 2-4 weeks before they go home, just enough time to get to know them and then they're gone.

It's funny, though, because they all seem like my little brothers. I want to mother and take care of them in a platonic way. I got my first proposition the other day, but I couldn't really believe him and laughed it off and we're good friends. [see Propositions]

Letter. May 22, An Khe

Sometimes I get the most outrageously happy feeling about being here and seeing how the army works, how guys are in combat areas, war, etc. I can be sitting in a truck on a date (a recent date was moved to a convenient hospital jeep from an open jeep because it started to rain) just talking, because there's nothing else to do on a date in Vietnam, or go to a club and talk, or else I meet someone in the center whom I feel "sympatique" towards immediately, or I see grubby combat people coming back, and I'm just thankful that I had the crazy idea of coming here. I'll never be able to explain it—all I can do is try.

Talking about "dating" in a war zone may sound like an oxymoron, especially to the man humping through the jungle who hasn't seen a woman in six months. It certainly wasn't traditional at-home dating, but where there are men and women, they will find ways to get together. We were told by the Red Cross to date only officers, not enlisted men, which we of course ignored. As I say in my letters, any kind of date was difficult, but even more so with EMs. Another problem was that the men were constantly coming and going—on missions, reassigned, transferred home—or worse, killed.

Letter. May 29, An Khe

That photo is of a dinner party given by the division artists—young, intelligent, very nice and talented boys who have just finished putting together a portfolio about the 1st Cav with pictures they've drawn. They invited us to dinner to see some of their work. Four of us girls dressed up and went to their office where they had set up makeshift tables, turned-over wastebaskets served as chairs, a camouflage poncho liner for a tablecloth, and decorations of candles and a bottle vase of wild flowers. They had prepared C-rations for us and served them by opening the cans. C-rations are great—like opening a surprise package. It was a really beautiful evening—a quiet, dark cozy place, wonderful boys, great talks about art and none of the usual business with the guys trying to make an impression with witty small talk.

Letter. June 23, An Khe

It seemed like everyone I talked to irritated me, so I didn't speak to anyone. This was in a period of days when everything seemed awful for some reason. I was really hating everyone and wondering if I would ever make it through a whole year (I still do). But then that passed as all things do, and all has been good for the past week or so. It kind of goes in cycles of about two weeks when everything is good, and then one or two days come when I never want to see another person. Our emotions here seem to be very much on the surface and little stupid things affect us greatly and can ruin a really good day otherwise.

For instance, one day I was having one of my really good days when I loved everyone (after this bad period) and a guy I like who I hadn't seen in a while came up and said that he had heard from a friend of his that I was getting snobbish. Well, I should have just taken it with a grain of salt, but it really upset me and I cried a little, and I hadn't cried in a long time before I came here.

In writing about a sergeant from Michigan and a man from North Carolina. That's one of the good things about being here because I'm meeting tons of guys from different backgrounds who I never would have met otherwise. It's difficult, though, because there's so little to do, especially if you date an EM because we can't go to their clubs so you have to have a lot to talk about if you're going to get through the evening.

Letter. July 14, An Khe

Something very disrupting happened in Phan Thiet yesterday. The guy who was supposed to be our escort officer can't stand Red Cross girls. I had a huge argument with him about our purpose and whether we were worthwhile. He was rather obnoxious and rude, but what he said was true enough. He says that the guys don't like us coming out to LZ's and just talking to them for ten minutes, asking stupid questions about where they're from, etc., and that it's really frustrating to them. All of that may be true, but we think that for each guy who doesn't want to see us, there are at least two or three who are so happy to see an American girl who has volunteered to come and be with them. It's so hard to make them see that we're really here for them and that everything we do is for them.

The feeling I have for the guys over here is amazing—I love them all, I pity them, I admire them and want to do anything in my power to make it better for them here.

I especially love the grunts or infantry. They are the ones who are fighting and grubbing around and dying for everyone else and they have no choice. They're just put there and they're scared. They're just too darn young to be here dying and getting maimed for life. I could go on and on about the guys—I know it must get boring for you but to write about the programs we do would be monotonous for me. The programs are fun and sometimes rewarding, but it's the guys in the field I really love and want to talk about.

Letter. Oct. 1, Danang

Near the Center there is a group of Seabees who blast rocks in a nearby quarry daily at 12:00 and 5:00. We have a sign in the center telling the guys this happens.

The other day when the 5:00 blast went off I was walking through the center and this poor little grunt looked up at me, really startled and questioning and scared, and grabbed the table. I sort of shook my head at him to say it was okay and then I had to come back to the office because I nearly started to cry.

I had the strongest urge to just go up to him and put my arms around him and pat his head and comfort him. It sounds corny, but as I've told you before, our emotions are really on the surface here, and sometimes the feelings I get for these guys really surprise me.

Tape. Dec., Cu Chi

I'll tell you about R&R in Tokyo and Japan. I really didn't do too much. I saw several cities and buddhas and temples and stuff, but I went alone and I really didn't like being alone and I didn't meet anybody and I didn't make much of an effort. So I just spent most of the time sightseeing during the day and then I took great long baths. I must have taken 10 baths in six days, and showers also. I just slept a lot and I stayed three nights in a Hilton Hotel. It was fantastic.

Tape. Dec., Cu Chi

After I left Danang and came down here to Cu Chi, things were really miserable. I was in a really really bad mood for a whole month, and then finally I went on R&R to Tokyo.

While I was there I found out that I really missed this place and missed being with the guys and hearing about the war and being here when things were happening, and so I was really glad to get back. Before I went I thought that if anybody had said, okay, you can go home anytime you want now without losing face, I would have gone. But now that I'm back I'm ready to stick it out till the end and I think I'll be sad to leave even then.

Tape. Dec. 22, Cu Chi

One of my friends, Kenny, who just left gave me a whole box of perfume and powder just before he left. It was really nice.

Tape. Feb. 28, Cu Chi

A man who lived in the town where my father worked called him when he got home at my suggestion and they had lunch together.

I'm glad you had lunch with Joe. What he said about the guys really liking us over here, well, I'm sure that is true, but about them not minding that they can't date us—that really gets on their nerves sometimes because they see us going out with officers and going to officers' clubs and we don't go the EM clubs that often, and it really does bug them.

There is really only this one Radio Research EM club that I feel I can go to at ease. Even though we see the guys every day, there really isn't that much to say to most of them afterwards. The center at An Khe was great because you could talk to them easily and move around a lot, but going to a club here would just be kind of hard to talk to them for a long period of time.

My parents told me that they were going to Florida for a vacation because they needed to "get away from things for a while." I responded:

I know how you feel and I don't know why you should feel guilty. You know that the men are over here suffering, but somebody is always worse off than you. You have to get this attitude that it is just luck.

So they got the bad deal and they're out in the field and I'm back here, but still it's not that good for me. I know a lot of them feel guilty about it sometimes that they are not out in the field. You can't really do it because it's still bad no matter how it is. Sometimes even I feel guilty, like when I see that we aren't going out to visit them in the field, that we're sitting back here safe and sound, but you can just only do so much. Every guy over here can only do so much.

Letter. March 15, Cu Chi

I went through a hate-guys week, but I'm beginning to love them again now. Tonight I went to a place where they train promising EMs to be combat leaders. They take them out of their unit for nine days of training. They're really good guys—the best of the bunch—and I love sitting around talking to them like I used to in An Khe at the Center.

One day at the hospital I got into an absolutely wild and wonderful conversation with about ten guys about hippies and draft dodgers and the war, etc. They all agreed that protesters are doing it the wrong way, should write to congressmen, that they're chicken and a lot more.

Even though I'm getting tired and ready to go, I'm going to miss these guys and my relationship with them more than I can ever explain to you or anyone else except another Donut Dollie. All the pain, hurt, depression, fatigue are worth it for these guys. I haven't had this feeling of the great love for them for quite a while, but I do tonight and altho it sounds corny, I think it's the best emotion a person can have—this feeling of loving mankind (in this case it's the GIs in Vietnam).

We had a few false alarm mortars when I was with some guys tonight and the way they jump up or just stop dead what they're doing to listen makes me want to cry for them. And I told them so too. Almost every unit here is being hit and it just keeps going on and on. One company lost 80 killed, 10 wounded and 10 escaped. Another had 5 killed last night and 10 wounded from artillery from another company in the same unit called in by an RTO. Two or 3 other companies have bad casualties and it just feels like it's going on and on and getting no better.

I can't imagine leaving these guys and not riding on their tracks with them when they go out or meeting them with balloons and riding the trucks or tracks back when they come in, or getting up at 4:00 am to serve breakfast to the Wolfhounds going out, or serving lunch to a line of grubby slightly wounded men who are back in without their units for a few days of rest before they go back out to their company which just lost ten men, or just talking to a guy in the hospital who says over and over in a joking way but dead serious, "I don't want to go back out there, I'm scared."

I really know very little about them, their backgrounds, but I feel so close to them. I can't always talk to them for a long time without running out of things to say, but I know them. And then sometimes I find one I feel like I could talk to for hours. They'll risk their life for a buddy or shoot an officer or a guy in the back if he's so bad he's endangering their lives, or they'll stamp a Wolfhound crest in a dead gook's forehead or save a gold tooth for a war trophy—and they love dogs and children. What can I say. You've heard it all before. Enough, enough.

Last tape. April, Cu Chi

This last week I've pretty much been going around seeing people. Not really saying good-bye because I hate to tell guys that I'm going home and they have to stay over here.

I haven't thought much about how I feel about going home. I just have been so busy, I haven't had a chance to sit down and let myself think for more than 15 minutes at a time, because I find I get rather depressed if I think too long about anything. I think about coming home, which is good, but I am really going to miss it here.

A few nights ago we had a rocket land about 50 yards from our hooch, practically right on top of the commanding general's desk. He wasn't there, fortunately. Nobody got hurt but it burned a hole in the general's office and all the other offices around there, and the scrolls that they usually give the girls when they go away were burned.

So at the good-bye dinner at the general's mess, instead they gave me a yearbook of the 25th Division and it's really cool. I'd rather have that than the scroll so it's lucky for me, in a way, that it burnt.

That was really pretty scary, though. We had an awful close one, and a huge fire resulted from it. Naturally I was crawling on the floor trying to get under the bed which I couldn't fit under. And the other day we had a monsoon that started with all sorts of thunder. At the first thunder crack I was scared to death and I ducked behind a desk. I can just see me at home. I wonder if I'll really act that way, the way they say the guys do when they go on leave. But whenever I hear a loud noise my heart starts thumping and I jump behind desks. It's really quite funny.

Nancy Caracciolo Warner described her mixed feelings about her year, feelings we all share.

I miss the emotional intensity I felt that year. Very few things in life now evoke the extremes of emotion that I felt on a daily basis there. I mean things like being so tired sometimes or so hungry, or so hot, or so cold, or so happy or so sad. The absolute extremes of every emotional or physical feeling that were constant.

My indoctrination came not from basic training since I was a civilian, but rather from the GIs themselves while in Vietnam. Living on base, we had little contact with the Vietnamese except

for mama-sans who cleaned our hooch and the people who worked in the recreation centers. Since my interest and focus was on the American men rather than having a cultural experience, I made little effort to interact with them, other than the day-to-day business.

However, I took on the attitudes of the men in many aspects of the war, including their feelings about the Vietnamese, part of which was that they can't be trusted—mama-sans by day, VC by night. And the lowest point came while I was stationed at Danang when a saying was going around—a saying that I used too—"Are gooks really people?"

Now I often find myself laughing with guys in our Vet Center group with that sick black humor of Vietnam. Others would gasp at our "insensitivity" but we understand what's behind the laughter.

Vietnam was a situation where the Vietnamese people were both our allies and our enemies—sometimes both at once. Since the enemy is always denigrated and turned into a monster (nips, krauts, slopes, yellow peril), it's almost impossible to learn to treat them as both real people and sub-humans.

War ain't pretty.

I don't remember trying to escape. Almost everything I did in my spare time I did with the guys, willingly. I played liar's dice in the officers' club, went to visit favorite units like the R&R unit at Cu Chi or the mechanics on the flight line, or I dispatched the NSA taxis in Danang and got a charge out of hearing the amazement when the guys heard a girl's voice, or I DJed for AFVN in Danang, or I went to a C-ration picnic with a combat photographer group at An Khe; I drank and danced at the officers' clubs; I welcomed guys in from the field or served them breakfast at 3:00 am before they went out. I don't remember ever sitting in my room by myself. Everything I did revolved around the men and I don't regret a minute of it.

On the other hand, to be honest, there were times when it was fun and relaxing to hang out with the other DDs in our hooch or to be with just one guy with whom I didn't have to be "on" all the time.

⚯

Emily Strange and the other girls at Dong Tam received a special invitation:

1245 Hrs

16 June 69

Girls,

It would be our extreme pleasure to entertain you for the afternoon or a portion thereof. Your presence would be a great morale booster. An air-conditioned hootch [sic], pleasant tapes, and perhaps a short tour of our facilities would be on the agenda.

Sincerely,

9th Signal

⚯

When I was at Danang, I would sometimes help out at the dispatch office for NSA taxis, where guys would call in asking for a vehicle to take them somewhere. The reactions to hearing a female voice varied greatly. Some just appeared to take it in stride, like they were Stateside. Others started stammering, sometimes after a long pause as they tried to figure out this phenomenon, forget why they called, ask who I was, etc.

The best was when the guy I was dating called, heard my voice and, without missing a beat, said "Hi, Nancy" and went ahead and requested the taxi. When I asked why he wasn't surprised, he said he never knew where I'd turn up.

WHO KNEW…

The games we'd play.
I was invited to sit in the cockpit of a flight taking us down to coast so
I donned the extra headset and enjoyed the chatter as well as the view.
Nearing our destination the pilot wrote down some flight information
And, with a twinkle in his eye, signaled for me to read it.
That was my clue the game was on.
So ah used mah best Southe'n drawl to ahdentifah ouwa aihcraft for the aihfield
and requested landing instructions.

NO response…

Their stunned silence was palpable, and the men in our cockpit collapsed in laughter.
Then the radio clicked, followed by a long pause and a disbelieving,
W-Would you repeat that, please……uh, M'am!

I did…breathlessly adding a touch of Marilyn Monroe.

They were literally hanging out the tower windows to wave to us when we landed.

J. Holley (McAleese) Watts
© 2004

There's a photo that I took in Vietnam that always makes me smile when I see it. It's of a guy I befriended who was a REMF at An Khe. Can't remember his job but he was definitely a REMF and glad of it. One day, as a joke he decided he wanted a war picture, so we went into the tall grass behind a building. He was dressed in full battle gear. I took a picture of him pointing into the distance...and so we labeled it "Point Man."

Point Man Skip in the "bush" at An Khe

We usually ate in the mess halls, except at Danang where we ate our dinner in the Officers' Club, a short walk from our villa. Strangely, I have virtually no memory of those meals.

The meals I do remember were the special ones with the men. When we went to the forward LZ's and firebases, we often served the meals in the chow line. I always chose to dish out the vegetable, encouraging the men to have at least one pea or one bean. Usually they acquiesced with a rueful semi-smile, but other times they flat-out refused. Afterwards we would sit and eat with them, hoping the officers wouldn't insist we sit in their area.

I always enjoyed the "C-ration picnics," as I called them much to the disdain of the men. Since we didn't have to eat C's every day, it became a treat. And although it was hard for the guys to believe, my favorite truly was ham and limas, better known to the men by an unprintable name.

I learned to play liar's dice at the Officers' Club at Cu Chi. We'd sit at the bar, throwing dice and lying for hours.

I also learned to drink stingers at Cu Chi—the bite of brandy mellowed by peppermint schnapps. I never remember getting drunk, but I suspect I must have.

A DD enjoying a C-ration picnic with the 5th of the 7th, 1st Cav at An Khe

I find it interesting to hear how the men viewed us, and also to remember how I felt. For instance, I've heard a lot of guys say how embarrassed they were to be so dirty, smelly, whatever, in our presence or when the nurses got them. It's hard for us to imagine, but when you think about their age and how they remembered themselves around American girls, I can certainly imagine that they'd like to have been more strac and just plain cool.

I never saw Maggie [Martha] Raye or got close to anyone famous, but we did have glamorous USO women and famous men do shows and visit in the hospitals when we too were visiting. My reaction was one of bemusement and maybe a teeny bit of jealously that they would get so much attention, but mostly I just understood that of course they would. I would have responded the same way if they'd come to visit me.

And besides, I knew I'd be there when they left— and I knew the guys knew it too.

There are two sets of veterans for me—the guys I knew in Vietnam and the ones I've met since who are so OLD!!! The first time I was sitting in a Vet Center group in the mid-80s, I blurted out, "But you guys are so old!" They pointed out to me that I was older too.

It was such a disconnect to me, though, to remember those cute young bewildered tough guys I loved so much and to think that these grey-haired men were the same ones. Unfortunately, I can't really make the transition in my mind—the ones I know now aren't the ones I knew then, and I don't mean that literally. They've changed so much, been through such pain, struggled with so many problems, whereas before all they had to worry about in Vietnam was staying alive and keeping their buddies alive too.

It's hard, if not impossible, for me to see the 19-year old in them and I regret that greatly.

Chris Noel, a cute vivacious blond, broadcast a much-loved radio program called "A Date With Chris" from the States and also visited the GIs in Vietnam from 1966-69. She has continued to work with and for veterans ever since.

Folks were hanging around the Hotel Washington in DC, back in the early days of these veteran gatherings, and I started rounding up people to go to dinner. Chris was sitting there by herself, so I suggested to the guys that we ask her to go with us, knowing that of course she'd be busy. But I asked and she said she'd love to. So about seven guys and Chris and I went to dinner in some funky Vietnamese restaurant. I said about two words the whole dinner and once again was glad to sit on the sidelines and watch her entertain. The guys loved it ("I had dinner with CHRIS NOEL!!") and she was great with them.

She's also great with the women who were in Vietnam—always asks us to come up on stage with her and is very respectful and just a neat woman. I only know her personal story from hearsay, but yeah, I'm a fan.

A couple of weeks ago during our discussion about Chris Noel, gene'o asked the question, "Does Chris Noel understand what she meant to the guys?" That started me thinking about writing about things I usually avoid. I can't speak for Chris Noel, of course, but Red Cross Donut Dollies were in somewhat the same category as morale boosters. People have asked, "What did Donut Dollies do," or "What was it like to be a Donut Dollie," and I usually dodge the question, at least until I know the person better or have the internal strength to formulate a coherent answer—and then deal with their response. So I'm going to give it a go now.

We were there to boost the morale of the troops, plain and simple, although nothing was really plain and simple in Vietnam. But what did we know or understand about our effect? Did we really have a clue? Although I was almost 25 when I arrived, older than most, and had traveled extensively, I was very naive, and amazingly, I remained naive throughout my tour. I think that had a positive as well as negative result. I don't think any of us really understood the effect that our presence—the presence of an American girl—had on the men. And I know now that those responses varied, although at the time I was in too much of a do-good fog to realize it. For the most part the guys we saw then, just as now, are the ones who wanted to talk to an American girl. They were invariably polite and very sweet. During my whole tour I had only one upsetting experience which I brought on myself by my own naiveté and ignorance. Sometimes the guys were coerced by their officers into participating in our silly programs, which we didn't like but could do nothing about, but even then they were nice, and usually got into the silliness with us.

My feelings at the time were of a tremendous compassion for the men because of what they were going through, as I understood it. If I had understood more then, or if I had known about PTSD, I don't think I could have continued to function. I had great admiration for the nurses who played both roles, that of care-taker and the ideal American woman, while knowing and experiencing much more of the pain than we did. We visited in hospitals and knew men who died, but it wasn't every day, 12-14 hours a day. Like you guys who were doing a John Wayne, I was doing a Florence Nightingale, recreation-worker style. I loved the guys, felt they loved us even though they didn't or couldn't always express it. I willingly wore rose-colored glasses—and still do to a great extent.

So that was then, this is now. In the intervening years, I've grown older and somewhat wiser about all this. I know now that it wasn't the innocent love-fest I imagined. For instance, a guy who became my best friend as he was recuperating at the Fort Knox hospital where I worked after I came back from Vietnam told me that whenever the DDs came to his firebase, he'd get as far away as possible because he didn't want the tease. Some, I think, resented our presence for other reasons which I can't really understand because I wasn't a young man in combat. I think they attributed bad motives to our presence because they couldn't understand why young girls like us would volunteer to be there. And boys will be boys, and girls are probably the preferred topic of conversation.

So back to gene'o's comment—does Chris Noel understand what she meant to the guys. Again, I can't speak for her, but the way I perceive things now is this. I wear my uniform on Memorial Day and Veterans Day at the Wall. I wear it to show that I was with you guys then and I'm still with you now. You were important then, and you are still important to me now. I also wear it because I'm proud to have been there, with you. I get various responses from the guys—almost all of them positive. During the early years of our (yours and mine) coming out, I heard several negative comments. It seemed like the guys had to get off their chest the bad things they thought about us. I really didn't want to hear it. Now, especially as a result of the Women's Memorial, the guys seem to understand more about why we women were there and what we've been through since. I get many thanks, kisses on the cheek, smiles, whoops of "there's a Donut Dollie," and much love. The ones that still don't get it don't tell me. I like to think that I understand in a way what an American woman in Vietnam meant to the guys, but like being in combat, I can never walk in those boots so I'll never really know. But what I would really like to have happen is that the guys understand how special they were to us, and how that love persists today, rose-colored glasses and all.

So that's one way of thinking about what was it like to be a woman in Vietnam, and whether we really understand. In my case, yes, but probably mostly no.

I had a wonderful year. I told a fellow Donut Dollie while I was there that it would be the best year of my life, and that has proven true. I had nothing terrible happen to me there—but that only means that I wasn't in any "real" danger other than mortar and rocket attacks, especially during Tet; I had no one I was close to die, although I knew men who died; I wasn't exposed to mass casualties or triage, although I visited frequently in hospitals. It was all relative. I loved being able to make the men laugh and forget the war for a moment. I loved feeling like I made a difference, even though I knew it was just my round eyes and the fact that I was there that counted.

The Special Ones

11

Our lives revolved around the men and they left an indelible mark on us, sometimes as a group and sometimes as an individual. The group could be a favorite unit, big or small, like the LRRPSs and R&R at Cu Chi, the Garry Owen Regiment at An Khe, or any Marine. The individual could be a friend we hung out with for weeks or someone we spent just five seconds with on a firebase or in the hospital—but we remember.

In this remembrance, René Johnson expresses the roller-coaster of feelings in Vietnam and the impact of one special man.

The Best of Times, The Worst of Times

That is what we were told to expect while we were in training for our job. Most days were really good days. In fact, most were great days!

One day Karen and I were scheduled to go to Duc Pho, and while there, to the Scout Dog unit. We weren't supposed to have favorites, but...I suppose we all did, and this was one of mine. They were all great guys, but one of the handlers, Curt, was special. Not in a romantic way, but just a soul-to-soul friendship. Usually we served lunch in the mess halls, but this time during our lunch break Karen had lunch with one of her friends, and I took a drive with Curt. Curt had gotten a jeep and we just drove around and around the base, talking about anything and everything, including his wife Nancy, why he'd gotten married, wondering if he would be the same man when he got home as his wife of only a few weeks had seen off. He had married someone he'd known only a short time, mainly because he did not want to go to Vietnam and have no one waiting for him back home. And he was wondering if he had done the right thing, for either of them. As we kept going past some of the areas, we noticed that the guys were starting to watch for us to come by, waving and cheering us along on our "road trip." As we went behind one of the boulders, Curt turned around and we drove in the opposite direction, just to confuse our "fans." It was a truly great day!!

After lunch, while Karen and I were programming in a mess hall behind the Scout Dog unit there was an explosion and we all hit the deck. It didn't sound like incoming or outgoing, so we were soon back on our feet, playing a game, getting the guys to laugh— doing what we were supposed to be doing, but hearing unusual activity just outside.

Not long afterwards, one of the other dog handlers came running in, pulled me aside and told me that Curt and two others had been badly burned in an explosion and medevaced out to Chu Lai. As we continued on to the other units, I know that my heart wasn't in it, but I remember consciously trying to hold onto that "Donut Dolly Smile" and go on as though it was a normal day.

By the time we finished there, it was time to go back to Chu Lai. I'd found out which hospital Curt was taken to and planned to ask the pilot to let me off there. But. There's always a "But." It had started raining, hard, and the aircraft were grounded except for dire emergencies. The only time in that year that I was weathered in was the one time that I simply had to get back to division headquarters. We were put up in an officer's quarters, and all night I kept trying to find out how Curt was with no luck. When we flew back to Chu Lai the next morning, I "told," not asked, my unit director that I was going to 27th Surg to check on Curt, and that I didn't know when I would be back. She didn't even blink; just said to keep her informed.

Curt's injuries were beyond severe. I couldn't recognize him in the room, even when he was pointed out by one of the nurses. He had third degree burns over more than 50% of his body and was not expected to live. A consequence of burns that I was not aware of was edema. Covered by the sheets, he looked like 400-pound person. A special plane was coming in from Japan to pick up the three of them, but there was no estimated time of arrival. I don't know how many hours I sat with Curt. He was given morphine regularly for the pain, before he could ask. He knew that I was there in the brief intervals that he was alert. By now, the plane was due to arrive early the next morning, but a very kind nurse had told me that he was not expected to be alive when it arrived. I had been talking to him, telling him how important it was for him to stay alive for Nancy, for whatever plans they had for the future. I stayed all night, and my unit director was fine with that, agreeing that our Saigon supervisors never needed to know.

In the instant we heard the sound of that explosion, one of the greatest days of my tour turned into the worst.

Afterward: Curt spent a very long time in the hospital in Japan before he could even be moved to the States, and then months at Brooke Army Hospital in the burn unit. I wrote regularly and until he could write himself, Nancy would write to let me know how he was doing, what progress was being made. In spite of his injuries, his altered appearance, the changes in what he would be able to do, that very young, very new wife never gave up on him, never let him down. And he never let her down. I visited them in 1971, and while I was there Nancy learned that she was expecting. Their daughter is named Amber René.

Jeanne Bokina Christie (nickname Sam) got hooked on flying when taken on short hops with friends as a high school student. Her love of flying and pilots carried over to Vietnam, especially the F4 pilots with whom she bonded at Danang.

Flyboys

F4 pilots were a mixed bag of personalities—cocky, arrogant, unapproachable to women and sweet, kind, giving, willing to listen to women. They were very protective and yet respectful of our space and our job. They were confident because of the control and adrenaline on which they thrived, doing their job to fly missions in a very expensive aircraft and survive the war.

I received an up-close tour of the F4s and had many a picture taken while sitting in one. One of the pilots, Tom, became my good friend when I was relatively new in country. He was a southern gentleman, mindful of his social manners but self-confident. He respected what we did as women in the war zone—always smile and listen and provide a touch of home in the crazy war zone. Another pilot, a Special Forces chopper pilot from my home state, would fly me to visit with Tom because it was too dangerous to drive me the few miles between locations. Tom had managed to get through the war without any real mishaps, and after he rotated home, we continued our friendship with letters. When I went home, he was the individual I went to see before heading home. He knew I had faced some real challenges but right off the bat said, "You are 10 pounds overweight and your head is a mess!" Who else would have been so frank and yet so perceptive. I trusted and respected his opinion and prepared to head home.

The rule was never date a married man… a geographic bachelor. JC, another F4 pilot, was a kind, respectful individual who listened when I talked. He was interested in hearing about what the DDs did and about the men we met out in the field or at work in the Center. Our conversation quickly transcended from the "Hi, where are you from" to real issues and how he was surviving the war. I was curious about his work, his plane, his abilities and perspectives about the war, about which he had an educated intellectual approach, a cultural perspective that was invigorating to me, not just the knee jerk reaction a cocky flyboy might have.

He, too, was a southern gentleman and his manners were always respectful. He touched my sealed-off sensitive side and made me laugh and sometimes cry. He even allowed me to be around on the day he returned from his 100th mission over North Vietnam to celebrate his time to return home to his friends and family.

Midway through my tour while at Danang I started dating a Navy dentist from Alabama... Alabama!!!! I barely knew Alabama existed except that since I'd been in Vietnam I'd discovered that there was a whole other section of the US which I hadn't been exposed to in my New Jersey upbringing and Colorado college.

Barry was a died-in-the-wool southerner, country music and all. He used to talk about country singers and not infrequently sing country songs to me, especially Hank Williams and Waylon Jennings. One night when we sat on the double lifeguard stand on China Beach, he sang Waylon's "It's Time to Bum Again" to me. ("Woman, you get meaner every day and your naggin' is hard to stand. So I'll pack my bags and be on my way, cuz it's time to bum again.") For some reason, I loved it. When Waylon died in 2002, I wrote Barry, and he said he'd thought about that night on China Beach, too.

I came to love country music. When I got back to the States I bought records of Hank Williams (who became my special favorite), Waylon, and Johnny Cash. I still think of it as a gift during those sweet innocent times when I first learned about country music.

Barry gave me a Montagnard bracelet which I always wear, inscribed with his dentist drill: "For Miss Nancy, Danang 1967, From Barry." In the intervening years, it's broken about five times. I've had it re-welded, and as the inscription has worn off through the years, he has re-inscribed it twice.

The lifeguard stand was still there when I went back to Vietnam in '93. I got some sand from China Beach and sent him a small bottle of it. He told me that even before he read my note, he knew exactly what it was and where it was from.

Some memories are sweet......

Don't Mean Nothin'

12

This expression was used, usually at the end of a story or discussion, to appear to dismiss something as unimportant when in reality it was so important that it had to be diminished. It also addresses the ambivalence and incomprehensibleness of the war.

Letter. May 2, An Khe

The way they talk about the war is strange. A guy came into the center who had just returned from the field, and the first thing one of the guys asked him in an undertone was whether anyone had gotten killed. Another guy I talked to said that after a week you joke about the danger and killing (unless it's personal) because that's the only way to live with it. It's true too. I find it much easier to joke about it than worry and fret when you can't do anything about it.

Another guy I talked to was 18 years old and talked like the 24-year olds whom I've talked to on my travels who have been around and thought a lot about it. I couldn't believe he was 18. He had enlisted because he believed in the war and is working in the hospital. He's been here seven months and now thinks the war is ridiculous and irrational. "You should believe in something strongly enough not to fight for it," he said. An interesting way of thinking and possibly true.

Tonight I was in the Center talking to some guys—all very young, 19-20, really boys—and they were telling me about things that happened with the enemy. They told me all this in a very dispassionate way, the way boys tell any kind of a story or the way they try to explain things to females. They didn't get worked up or deliberately tell these thing to shock me. It just sort of came up in the conversation—like when one guy was telling a story about a particular mission and specified by saying it was the time so-and-so "got it" and so-and-so got both legs blown off. Another guy hadn't heard about it—he knew them and he just sat there shaking his head while the other guy continued his story. And then after all this, one of them said, "This hasn't changed me. I'm going to go home and forget all this like it never happened. I'm still young and I'm going to have some fun." I just hope to God they can forget it, but it seems incredible they could.

Maybe I'm seeing a false side which they put up in front of me. I may be wrong in my interpretations of what I see in how they act. But this is how I see it now.

Letter. May 17, An Khe

One of the main topics of conversation is always how much longer someone has before they go home. Because they talk about it so much and I have so long, it makes a year seem interminable whereas otherwise I wouldn't worry about it. The guys who are going home are worried about what they're going to say when people ask about the war—and almost without exception they say they're just going to say they don't want to talk about it, not because it's so horrible, but because they can't begin to explain what it's like and, besides, they just want to forget it all and be civilians again. I don't envy them at all their first month at home. For most I think it will really be awful, judging from my vaguely similar experience of coming home from foreign travels.

When I talk to these guys, I keep trying to make generalizations and find common characteristics, but as time goes on, I find that they think entirely opposite on the same things. A couple of guys I was talking to were saying that even though they don't like it here, they wouldn't have given up their year here for anything. They've learned so much they never could have any other way. So I start thinking how great it is that the guys think like this, and then two days later I was talking to someone who really hates it here and can't see any good in it at all. He's an intelligent boy, so I got mad at him and told him to go home that night and think of as many reasons as possible that were good about being here and tell me. He was mad too (jokingly), so he did that and then came back and gave me two good things, the only things he seriously thought he'd learned here: 1) to appreciate home more, 2) that he would beat his kid up if he was ever stupid enough to talk about joining the army. What can you say or do except keep on trying to get them to see the good?

Some guys may say it's two wasted years, some say it may be wasted in a way, but they can afford to give two years to their country. They can talk so calmly about their best buddy getting killed a few days ago, or their brother being killed, and then they become like avenging furies in the field with the VC. Many of them hate all Vietnamese and think we should pull out now—that one American life isn't worth giving for these wretched people. Other guys say we have to stay. Some guys don't condemn the anti-Vietnam marchers (the same one who said two years isn't much to give for your country), and others think everyone should be drafted. They all like to hear about pro-Vietnam demonstrations.

Letter. Aug. 28, Danang

That article you sent me about the riots at home and how the Negro guys say they feel safer here than at home is really true. I've talked to lots that are really worried about going home.

Tape. Jan. 12, Cu Chi

It's good to hear [my brother] Billy's in such good shape and still happy about coming over here. He said that he's not so sure about the war over here. I had a big long talk with somebody the other day about the war. Everybody seems to realize that we shouldn't be here. It's really stupid and the only reason we stay now is because we committed ourselves. Those EMs we were talking to said that we have to stay now so that the guys who died haven't died in vain. I don't know if I can agree with that, but that's what they really think. There's the parking lot theory about what to do about Vietnam where you take the good Vietnamese and put them on an island and then you turn Vietnam into a parking lot.

There was a guy here the other night who was knocking the kids in the field. He is a major and he was saying they were chicken and they've got to be forced to fight and things like that. I got really mad about it because these guys—I've never seen them in the field in a firefight, but they often talk to me in the hospital about how they don't want to go back to the field, and they're scared—they really are—but they do the job and I think it's great because they're fighting here for these people and in spite of what that guy said, I don't think these Vietnamese people are that great. I really don't like them, but I only see the point of view of the guys who have seen their buddies killed. I was talking to an EM the other night who said that he liked them and he was upset that I don't. I only see the bad side—what the guys say. I don't see the good side.

One of the most poignant flashback stories I've heard was from a veteran I met many years ago in DC when I persuaded him that there were enough tickets to get him into the very first DMZ to Delta Dance.

He's a salt-of-the-earth kind of guy—the kind of person we'd like our daughters to marry. Through the years I learned some of his story. One of the pieces that touched me most was when, after telling me about his wife who didn't want to hear about Vietnam, he told me about finding himself one day walking along a highway in Ohio...walking point.

He was taken to a VA hospital where they hadn't heard of PTSD, hospitalized for a couple of days and let go. Never got any help for years. Only after his wife left him and he came to DC for Veterans Day did he finally go for help. And even now he won't go to the Vet Center because he says there are others who he says need help more than he does.

But I think about this nice man, trying to do his best for his wife and three kids, be a good upstanding citizen...and finding himself walking point along the highway. And then not being able to get help....

The pain isn't over for them. I talked to a guy today who told me about how he was in a McDonald's in California just a couple of weeks ago wearing a Vietnam veteran hat when a woman in line asked, "How many babies did you kill?"

Feelings of War

13

As I expressed at various times in letters and tapes home, like the men I too felt ambivalent about the war and my being there. Now I clearly know the war was wrong, but it wasn't so clear when surrounded by men who were in the midst of it.

Letter. May 2, An Khe

Last night an NCO I've been going out with took me out to the perimeter and told me all about the security this base has. It's really fantastic and equally fantastic to think that with all our technology and equipment we can't win this stupid war. It's hard to be here and think it's wrong. I can see why the guys fighting believe in it and really hate the VC and even the Vietnamese, but I still have my doubts. Captains and majors I've talked to about it believe we're getting somewhere and the people want us, etc., etc. I can't really tell unless I talk to the people, and that's impossible, so......

Letter. June 23, An Khe

One more thing I meant to tell you about before—it's just a little thing but it really touched me. You remember that day I told you about when we went out to the airstrip to give Kool-Aid to a unit of guys who were coming in from the field for one day and then going right back out. While we were waiting there with them in the hot sun, there was one guy who was curled up under a truck in the shade trying to sleep. He wore glasses and looked like the kind of guy who belongs in a classroom studying and certainly not fighting a war. It was so pathetic and rather sickening. In spite of everything they say and everything you see over here to justify the war, I often think as some guys say that all of it's not worth one

American life. These guys are so young and they don't belong here grubbing in the dirt and rain, eating C-rations, when they should be home in school or with their wives or in a decent productive job. I just don't see how they can ever readjust to the normal way of life again.

I can't seem to get my thoughts straightened out about the war, and I don't know if I ever will.

Tonight a C-130 crashed. It's a troop carrier and it had about 50 people on it. It crashed on take-off because it didn't get up in time. They told us about it when I was working in the Center, and the original reports were that 100 people were on it and only 16 got out and one Red Cross girl who was on it was blinded. For some reason it really hit me—it wasn't like hearing about a company in the field getting wiped out, which is even worse—but I just started crying in the back office. I kept thinking about those poor people caught in the burning plane, wondering how many I knew, and then thinking, "I'm going home, I don't want to take any more chances, I'm going home." Then later reports came in. The Division photographer was there taking pictures and he said almost everyone got out. So, since I wanted to believe it, I did, and went back out into the Center with a bright, cheerful smile. The final report (so far) is that about 20 got out, the Red Cross girl is okay, and 34 GIs and Vietnamese (about 10) were left in it when it exploded.

Letter. July 14, An Khe

Today I went out in the field again and it was a very good and a very bad day. I was in a beautiful mood and had a lot of fun, but for the first time the war really began to get to me because as we were driving around the LZ, we saw a bunch of guys in field gear either about to go out or having just come in. So we jumped out of the vehicle to talk to them and found out they were from one of my favorite units—really fun guys. It turned out that they were about to go out to help another company in the unit who were involved in a firefight. So these guys, three platoons, were going out, and right after we talked to them the choppers came in to take them out. Then about an hour later we heard reports about them that there were already six killed and 20 or more wounded. It really gave me a sick feeling to know that probably some of the guys I had just been talking to were now dead. How can you ever justify a war?

This is being written on this [a small piece of paper] because I'm at the swimming hole without paper and suddenly inspired to write.

You know when I first came over here I wasn't sure how I would react to the war but I kind of thought I would grow to realize the necessity for it. But the more I see and hear about the guys getting killed (there's been a lot of fighting recently) the more I think that it's a stupid thing to say that we have to keep on fighting so that the guys who are already dead won't have died in vain. I figure the sooner we pull out and the fewer guys are killed the better. These guys are all so young and so many of them are being killed in such a rotten way. It's really strange to be sitting with three or four 19- or 20-year-olds and hear them talk about a fight they were in and the guys who got killed and how lucky there were to get out. It's just not right that they should have had to be lucky to be alive. They shouldn't have been forced to take the chance in the first place. They don't belong here. They belong at home with their girls and their motorcycles doing all the wild things guys do. I met a really nice guy the other day who draws really well, is soft-spoken and shy. He told me that he has been in a reformatory for about 2 ½ years of his life. It's so amazing to meet people like that who I would never meet otherwise. No matter what these guys are like at home, here they're all equal because all they want to do is survive. And yet often they get killed trying to save a buddy they loved and couldn't let die alone.

Letter. Aug. 28, Danang

You remember I said that I was waiting for the first time that a guy I knew got killed. About a week ago it happened. It wasn't anyone I knew very well—I had just met him once. He was a pilot and at this party he sang a bunch of songs he had written, satires on the war. He was a really nice guy that everyone liked, and then two days later he was killed while flying a mission. I just can't imagine what it does to these young kids who see their buddies getting killed one right after another. It just tears them up more than they'll ever be able to or want to express. God, I hate this stupid war.

Letter. Oct. 1, Danang

This whole war is the most disgusting and degrading thing that can happen, but even so it really brings out the best in men. You hear some wonderful stories about things guys do for their buddies in the field—like the officer from the south who hated Negroes, and had a Negro sergeant working under who was a good man, but still he was a Negro. So then the sergeant got shot and they found the officer sitting with him and cradling his head in his lap until he died.

I write you over and over again how I wish they'd just do anything to stop this stupid war and I really think it, and then I read in the paper or talk to a guy who is a real pacifist and I get so mad that they would pull out after everything we've put into this stinking country. It would be total negation of everything we believe in and have been fighting for for the past five years. And yet when I talk to the guys in the hospital and other places about what it's like in the field, I'd just give anything to end it all.

Those were my letters about my feelings about the war while I was there. In emails I wrote later, my ambivalent feelings became clearly against the war, but equally strongly in support of the men no matter how they thought about the war, which was, of course, how I felt while I was in Vietnam.

I went over in April '67 and within months wrote a letter home strongly questioning our involvement. I developed a strong dislike for the military, due in part to its leaders. Of course, some were wonderful, but bad leadership there got people killed, not just fired. I was ambivalent about fraggings. And I was well aware of prostitution and drugs. And then there was the argument about whether juicers or druggers were better or worse.

These are issues which may have become stereotypical, especially to those who weren't there, but to me they were very real and contribute to my continued ambivalence about enjoying my tour under such confusing circumstances

In 1970 I was living in San Francisco, "trying to find myself" while working as a secretary for an insurance agency. One day as I was walking in the business district in my super-secretary outfit, a guy handed me a flyer about an anti-war march coming up that weekend. I said, "I know about it," and he said pleasantly, "So you'll be there." I said yes.

I went, not knowing if I was going to be a spectator or a marcher, stood on the sidelines for a while, feeling very conflicted as various people and groups walked by. Then a group came by chanting, "Ho Ho Ho Chi Minh," and it crystallized for me why I hadn't been able to join the march. Although I desperately wanted the war to stop, I couldn't join "the other side." Intellectually and personally I knew that others in the anti-war movement wouldn't have agreed with that small group, but I felt it would have been a betrayal to have joined.

That and other experiences have led me to where I am now which is to try to focus on the people rather than on their political beliefs.

When I've talked to high school students with other veterans, the students were far more interested in the "war" stories than mine. Maybe it was because of my presentation which was mostly about PTSD.

I've always found it hard to explain what we did, and I'm afraid I often don't try. The only women they know anything about are nurses. Donut Dollies are an unknown mystery to them (as they are to many Vietnam veterans). In the face of the men telling their "war stories," my stories of playing games sound just stupid and frivolous.

Afterwards, all the questions and private conversations are with the men, from both the male and female students. Heaven knows, I don't expect kudos, but it's very unvalidating. I end up feeling like I offered a personal gift which wasn't acknowledged, let alone appreciated.

One time I was at a class and at some point I said something about not asking dumb questions of the vets. I can't remember the context exactly but at least in my mind it had to do with not asking how many people they killed. I noticed one of the students smiling at his teacher. I later learned that their teacher had told them there were no dumb questions.

Maybe it depends on how you define dumb—maybe I should have said, invasive or personal. Or maybe Vietnam is just a touchy subject for me.

I've talked to high school students about four times and hated it every time. I don't know why I keep doing it—something about growth—but I probably won't do again.

You know, as much as I wanted to go back—longed to go back—I'm glad I didn't. It wasn't just that my brother was killed there three months after I got back, but more because just having a break of home life, being back in the world and into reality would have made going back and seeing the futility of the war, the unimaginable damage being done to the men which I couldn't see as clearly while I was in the midst of it—well, I could see it but I couldn't let myself think about it—how could I have gone back and been the cheerful, relatively naive girl I'd been on my first tour.

When I saw the movie *Hamburger Hill,* I could see the seeds of PTSD being sown in the men, their false dreams of coming home. I could anticipate the disillusionment and pain they were going to find back in the world. That's what I think I would have felt and seen had I gone back.

Danang

14

Danang, my second assignment, was a mixed blessing. I hated leaving the Cav but as it turned out, I loved the Marines. However, I didn't love our living situation which separated us from the men because we lived in the city rather than on base. But we were with the Marines which made all the difference.

Letter. Aug. 28, Danang

Well, I guess it's high time I wrote you. I haven't wanted to write before because things were so bad. Now I'm gradually getting resigned to the boredom of this place and the fact that nothing will ever be as good as the Cav again. I've got about a hundred and one gripes about this place which I guess I might as well air first. Everything is so organized that it's almost like a 9 to 5 job except that a job in Vietnam could never be really boring, especially as long as there are guys around. Another thing which is really bad about this place is that we live in town which means that instead of walking out your door and seeing all sorts of great GIs or Marines, you see grubby Vietnamese people riding their bicycles all over the dirty road. I really miss seeing the guys all the time wherever I go. Also, I hardly can date EMs because it's really difficult for them to get into town, and so all we date is officers which gets to be a real drag.

Also it's really hard to get to know the guys and have lots of friends in the Center the way I did in An Khe because the guys don't stay around long enough. Almost all of them who come in to the Center are about to go on R&R or just coming back or in for a couple of days to fix their finances or something and then they go back out to the field for another couple of months. Also we hardly ever get out into the field because the Marines are so afraid something is going to happen to us and they don't want to be responsible, or else they don't think females belong in a war and don't think we would be good for the morale. It's so darn frustrating to have guys come into the Center from these really remote places where they never see girls for three or four months and they say to us, why don't you ever come out to see us, and all we can say is we're dying to but "they" won't let us. Things might be better now though because we're hoping to get clearance for a few new places, which would mean more field stops and trips out of this grubby city.

We have a little Center down at the airport where we see guys going on R&R and going home. When I'm there, every now and then I have to shake my head and make myself realize that there are Marines who really are going home. These are guys who have spent 13 months in the field up at the DMZ where the worst fighting is going on and I just can't believe that men actually do make it in one piece and go home again. I just want to say to each of them, how did you ever make it. We hear so much about whole companies getting killed or you meet a guy who has been in four platoons and he's the only one left out of all four or a guy tells you about a fight he was in when he saw all of his buddies falling around him, and it just doesn't seem possible that that one guy managed to stay alive.

Another really feeble thing about this set-up here is that we have to drive a half hour to work every day and therefore can't go back in the middle of the day. If it weren't for the Marines who are really good guys (actually what boys over here in combat units especially aren't great!) The Marines are great because they are almost all grunts which means they're the underdogs and having the rottenest time over here and that's why I love them the best.

The only other really good thing here is that we have mama-sans to clean up our house and wash our clothes and polish our shoes and everything. It really is a luxury—almost like living at home!

I have a picture I took outside the rec center in Danang of a group of Marines, one in civvies. I kind of ran into them there, a

platoon/squad with their officer (the one in civvies who had been called back from the States) because they/he had been charged with some kind of "atrocity." My memory of this is very vague, but I was quite taken with them as a cohesive group, joking and just loosely hanging out with their LT. Just a bunch of nice guys, which is why I took their picture. But there was this strange reason as to why he had come back to Vietnam which is what I'm not clear about. Just one of those strange memories which have greater meaning later, except that the fog of war colored it then and time obscures it now.

Once a Marine

15

How do you explain a Marine? The expression "Once a Marine, Always a Marine" is strongly imbedded. A Marine will say there are no ex-Marines or former Marines. They remain Marines throughout their lives. And, yes, Marine is always capitalized.

In these letters and emails I try to puzzle it out—the difference between soldiers and Marines, between the officers and EMs, between the Marine image and reality—and the over-riding love and compassion I felt for them all.

The distinction between soldier and Marine was brought home to me when I was transferred from the 1st Cav to the Marine Corps. One day after I'd been transferred from the 1st Cav to the Marines, we DDs were waiting for a chopper to take us somewhere. I looked into the sky wondered out loud where the "bird" was. The Marines looked at me like I was slightly daft until one said with only-partially concealed scorn, "She's been with the army."

Another time, very early on in Danang, I did what we DDs always did—wave and call out hi to any GI we saw along the way. So I called out, "Hi, soldier" (I can't really believe I actually said that since it seems so WWIIish), but I remember because I was given a dismissive look by the Marine and was quickly educated by the other Donut Dollie. "They're Marines, not soldiers."

Letter. Aug. 28, Danang

I talked to a guy yesterday who hadn't talked to an English-speaking girl in ten months. It's hard to understand what it must be like for those poor guys in the field.

Letter. Oct. 1, Danang

I've been talking to the men and asking them why they joined the Marines instead of another service. Most of them say because they had to come into the service anyway or they wanted to come in and the Marine Corps is the best, as everyone knows. The guy I played cards with on the floor said the officers in the Corps are like little gods. There is very little closeness between officers and the men like there is in the army, even though they fight together. He said that they are told that officers are really just far above them and must be shown all kinds of respect, etc.

Letter. Oct. 8, Danang

Apparently the Cav is moving north to take over positions which the Marines held a little south of here so that the Marines can go up to the DMZ, the poor guys. They are so scared. I talked to a guy the other day who is going up there and he says he's been through three complete platoons and he is the only one left in them all.

Ginger just came into the office and told me that three guys from that unit that's moving north just came in here and asked if they could leave their gear here until they come back down because they're due to rotate home on the 20th. They said that if they didn't make it back down, we could keep their stuff. Can you imagine being in a position where you would need to say something like that?

The other day I went down to a place south of here which we go to every week for a regular run, and I had a really great time. First of all I met a couple of very nice and funny Aussie guys. The best part of all was that we got to see B Company 1/5 which is probably the most famous Marine company of all. They have been in some really bad fighting which wiped out about half their company or more and they're the ones who have moved out who the Cav is replacing. You know the picture of the guys running off a chopper advertising savings bonds and they're called the Danang Patrol. Well, that's these guys. In spite of their reputation which they're very proud of, with us they're just regular people, falling all over themselves to see girls and then trying so hard not to say anything bad and slipping occasionally and apologizing and being very embarrassed. When they get home they'll be big and tough again, but here we get to see them as no other girls will ever see them again and they're really beautiful.

Letter. Nov., Danang

We girls were talking about how different the Marine officers are. They really don't seem to have as much cool as the army officers, especially when it comes to interacting with girls. But the Marines—the enlisted Marines—are just beautiful. They're really good guys. A lot of them talk about regretting that they came into the Marine Corps, but I think that they'll lose that or they won't think or say that when they go home, because they're really proud to be Marines. So much of the time they're so defenseless because they don't have the equipment, they don't have the weapons, and they can't fight the way they were trained. These places like Dong Ha and Con Thien. They send jets up there, phantom jets, and they bomb all over the place, but they can't get them because they're buried. It's so discouraging for the Marines, and when they do make contact, it's not the contact they wanted to make. It's because they're ambushed or because the VC decided they would get them.

It's really tragic to see them come into the center all dirty and grubby, and they just sit and stare at us which you read about–all these guys can do is sit on their hills, with the artillery just coming in from the other side of the DMZ, but they can't get that artillery because of where it's coming from. They can't believe they're talking to a girl, a real girl, and they can't understand why we're here. It was like this down in An Khe too, but not the same. The Marines are, surprisingly enough, much shyer than the guys from the army. They don't talk as freely and they don't joke around as much. You really have to make an effort and it's a lot harder. In lots of ways, I'm glad I'm leaving because the effort is much greater, but I'll be so sad to leave the Marines. I'll be sad to go down south because the war is definitely up north—that's where everything is happening. But I'm really lucky and glad that I did get a chance to see the Marines. Now I'll know what people are talking about when they talk about the Marines and the Marine Corps.

The Marines have no equipment at all. These guys come back here and they have no money because they haven't been able to get their pay for the last two or three months and they can't even buy things like razor blades. One guy I knew got back from R&R—a good friend of mine that I met when I first came up here. He used to buy me lunch, but now he didn't have any money so I took him to lunch and gave him my cigarettes.

Marine Corps birthday, November 10, was a really big deal. Without telling them the reason, at my request Ginger, the UD, had persuaded Saigon to delay my transfer to Cu Chi, saying I was desperately needed in the unit until after said date so that I could go to the party, even though I expressed some trepidation in my tape home.

Tape. Dec., Cu Chi

Usually these Marine parties are not great because the men are rather lecherous and I was really worried about this. We had to go because it was a big deal and we had been invited, so I went with a few other girls and it turned out to be great. I sat myself down next to a great big man who reminded me of Uncle Beanie. He was very nice and sort of protected me from all the other men who came over, so I could just sit there and enjoy it. The men were so happy and so wild and at about 9 or 10, they pulled out these champagne bottles—somebody said they had gotten 200 champagne bottles—and they all started popping the corks at once. It was really a beautiful party and I'm very glad I went. One great Marine party.

Letter. Dec. 15, Cu Chi

I've been really impatient with everyone and Saigon in its wisdom has decided to send me TDY to Danang for a week in two days which is great. I can't wait to go back. Even tho I probably won't still know anyone, I'll be with the Marines again and I LOVE them.

My over-riding memory about *Dispatches*, the book by Michael Herr, is the affection he had for the Marines, saying in part that they were different than the soldiers. It seems like virtually everyone who has spent time with both branches (I was with the 1st Cav, Marines, 25th Inf. Div.) says the same thing.

Interestingly, that difference doesn't seem to engender opinions that they are tough brutes but rather the opposite. I don't think that all of those softer feelings are due just to the observer but must come from the character of the men as well. David Douglas Duncan's photos in *War Without Heroes* demonstrate this.

An observation of mine is that Marines are highly trained to do the right thing. In social, civilian, domestic settings that correctness can be exhibited in extreme politeness and stiffness. On the other hand, all the toughness training didn't always translate well into some "social" gatherings, especially if they hadn't seen a female in months. The army, on the other hand, had more access to females and Donut Dollies, especially the Cav who flew us to a lot of forward areas.

Tosh Geraci Saunders happily surrounded by Marines at Danang

I Love Marines

16

Email written to a veteran group.

I love Marines. I also love the 1st Cav, the 25th Infantry Division, and other miscellaneous folks I wasn't attached to. But I LOVE Marines. As anyone who has ever had the privilege of hanging out around them (e.g., Michael Herr) will tell you, they are different. As any woman who has had the pleasure of working with them will tell you, they are shy, reserved, tongue-tied, sweet, pathetic, deprived, grubby, unsure of themselves—generally just puppy dogs. When they came into the recreation center in Danang, we had all we could do to get them to talk to us—shyness and awe overcame them. They'd just stand at a distance and watch.

Some of my favorite Marine stories—nothing earth-shaking—just the little incidents which make up a Donut Dollie's life in Vietnam.

I was walking through a group of probably 150 grunts sitting at tables outside (I can't figure out where it could have been—maybe Red Beach?). Every table was full of army guys (soldiers), but I noticed one table with 3 guys with Marine covers [Marine-speak for hats]. I walked over and said kind of under my breath, "Don't you guys feel outnumbered?" Quick as a flash, one of them came back with, "What do you mean, there are 3 of us!" I have since learned that they are taught this sense of superiority from the first day of boot camp, and they sure had learned the lesson.

I was sent back to Danang TDY (oops, TAD) for a week after I had been stationed there for 3 months. I was so happy to be back among the Marines that I made a huge sign (about 20 feet long) that said, I LOVE MARINES. I drew it on a long piece of brown paper on the floor in the middle of the rec center and before I could finish it, Marines and many others had written all over it, mostly just saying their name and unit, but with other variations as well. My favorite was the one which said, "God is a Grunt." After I got back to the world and was working at the hospital at Fort Knox, I was asked to speak to the local Red Cross chapter about my work in Vietnam. I showed them the sign and one little lady asked what that meant, "God is a grunt." I tried to explain what a high compliment that was, but I don't think I got the point across to this Bible-belt group of ladies.

Although I have traveled through numerous countries, including Italy, Turkey, Morocco, etc., the one and only time I have ever been pinched was in the Stone Elephant Officers' Club by a Marine officer....

At the Freedom Hill recreation center with another sign on the wall, written on by the guys.

Hospitals

17

Visiting in hospitals was voluntary, not a required part of our job. My hospital visits in Danang had a searing impact on me, giving me some of my most vivid memories of my tour. We never went on a ward without visiting every man in every bed. As you can imagine, it was very hard—the hardest thing I did—but rewarding.

Letter. Aug. 28, Danang

We visit the hospital three times a week for three hours each time and it's really interesting although tiring. We don't go into any wards where the guys are really bad but we do see guys who have been shot up or had legs amputated. Just yesterday I was talking to a guy whose leg was amputated and I didn't realize it for the first five minutes because we usually don't ask them what's wrong and it's safer to look just at their face so you don't see anything too embarrassing or sickening. So anyway, I didn't realize he was an amputee and he was really friendly and nice, much more outgoing than a lot of the guys in there, and then I finally realized it and I was really amazed. I didn't say anything about it but was just more careful about saying things about doing sports or something. All the girls say that the amputees are often the most cheerful and friendliest which absolutely amazes me because I would be so nasty and feel so sorry for myself that I wouldn't even talk to anyone.

Letter. Oct. 8, Danang

I really enjoy seeing the guys in the hospital because they're usually so nice to you and seem like they're glad to see you whether they are or not. I met a really interesting one yesterday who was only 21 (he'd gone to Dartmouth for a year) with very off-beat ideas. He was interested in me and the way I thought about things, and he said a really nice thing, too. He said, "How can you go around and see so many guys and yet always seem so personal?" That's really a compliment because it means I'm doing my job well, even when it can seem so hard.

One time was when I was on the ICU ward in Danang, a nurse asked me to talk with a guy who had been badly burned and was totally covered with bandages, eyes and all. I went over to him and tried to talk, but I've never been good at talking without getting a response which for him was not possible. So I went to the other DD, Ginger, and said, "I can't do it. Will you please talk to him?" As I walked away I heard her talking with him in her soft southern accent and knew she was the right person.

Another time I was visiting in the Marine ICU with another Donut Dollie. After I little bit, I said to her that I had to leave, I just couldn't take it. Leaving was very much against our code. We went to the nearby USO cafeteria and sat silently at a table drinking a coke. I was feeling terrible because I'd walked out on the men. Then a guy walked by and quickly and quietly said, "I just want to thank you girls for being here" and walked on. We were rarely thanked—didn't expect it, didn't need it in words, and that particular time I didn't think I deserved it...but I needed it and have treasured it.

Emily Strange experienced similar feelings about a particular hospital visit.

PLEASE FORGIVE ME
for not remembering your name

i know it is here somewhere on the West Wall
probably around panel 20

i remember your face, your smile
as you showed me the picture of your wife and new baby

i remember how they teased the new papa-san
as you danced around that desolate firebase laughing

i remember walking into ICU
as they unwrapped the gory stump that was your leg

and i remember my sorrow when the nurse whispered,
"expectant - he was already in a body bag
when the medic noticed slight breathing"

PLEASE FORGIVE ME
for not staying

i wanted to hold your hand and tell you
to hang in there for your wife and new baby

but the nurses and doctors surrounded you
trying to keep you alive

and i would have only been in the way
so i told the nurse i would check on you later

PLEASE FORGIVE ME
for not returning

i just did not want to know
that another wife would receive that knock on the door
confirming her worst fears

i couldn't bear to know that another child
would grow up having never known his Father

101

for i had an early take off the next morning
to fly to another desolate firebase
to laugh and dance with other soldiers
before they too were killed

PLEASE FORGIVE ME

©1989

Here is Emily

Nurses

18

On some bases we shared quarters with the nurses. In others we barely interacted, except perhaps when we visited in the hospitals. At An Khe we shared barracks with the nurses, meaning we shared a common bathroom, dayroom and yard. I have no memory of ever even saying hello to a nurse—not deliberately. It just didn't happen or it didn't leave a memory. I can speculate on reasons why—defensiveness on our part because of our lightweight jobs in comparison to theirs. They were doing serious, life-saving, wonderful work. We Donut Dollies were playing games with the men and flying around to forward areas. You can see why they might have thought that we and what we did were pretty lightweight and inconsequential.

I like to think I would have done things differently. There might not have been enough time or energy, but I like to think that when I saw a nurse in the bathroom as we washed our faces, I'd have smiled at her and asked how she was doing. I might even have asked about a patient I'd visited in the hospital or how she'd done when the C130 crashed on the airstrip. I like to think that if the nurses I've gotten to know in DC had been there, I'd have seen the love and beauty in their tired faces and felt empathy instead of just getting on with my day.

I like to think that when the nurse in the NSA hospital asked me to talk with the badly burned blinded man, she recognized that I had something to offer him that she felt unable to provide at that moment. I like to think that when she saw me tear up, she didn't think I was too naive for this job but rather that we had a hard time coping too.

I think it would have been very different for all of us—well, maybe not very different, but we'd have felt some of the understanding and caring which we feel for each other now. As I've become good friends with a nurse in DC, we've remarked that we each have some of the qualities of the other—nurse and Donut Dollie—that we brought to our two maybe-not-so-different jobs.

I don't consciously carry a lot of guilt. In fact, very little. But after you've done 2-3 hours of mental health research tests primarily directed at nurses, that tends to raise the guilt level a little bit...especially if you think too hard about the fact that you wore a little blue dress and flew around playing games and laughing with the cute guys...instead of grubbing it out for unending hours surrounded by blood and pain and despair.

Breaking Rules

19

The Donut Dollies often had very different feelings than the men about being in Vietnam, whether it had to do with wanting to leave, stay, extend the tour, or simply survive the experience. Breaking Red Cross rules could have dire consequences, but now the stories can be told. After all, what are they going to do? Send me to Vietnam?

In this email to the vet group, I describe my, and probably most of the girls', feelings.

I wasn't afraid of chopper crashes; I wasn't afraid of snipers; I wasn't afraid of being over-run although I worried occasionally about sappers; I wasn't afraid of mortars, although when the rockets started during Tet, that was unnerving. I wasn't afraid of a mess hall full of men; I wasn't afraid going to an isolated firebase and being one of two girls among hundreds of men.

But what I was afraid of was being sent home.

We broke the rules. We ALL broke the rules. The Red Cross had very strict rules. Breaking rules could be missing a curfew, illegal trips or plane rides (at least one girl snagged an F4 ride), drinking in uniform, smoking dope, and many more infractions. Dating enlisted men was discouraged (although several girls married EMs) and married men a no-no (although we didn't always know if someone was married). Being out of uniform could have qualified except that after a week or so in country, we all realized that our baby blue dresses needed more than the Red Cross supplied. Hats and scarves of various kinds were produced, and whatever shoes stayed on comfortably were acceptable (loafers for me).

Doing any of those things could be a quick ticket home. We dreaded "Saigon," i.e., our bosses—the honchos—in Saigon who came periodically for inspection visits. Although we signed up for a year tour, we could have chosen to go home at any time. I don't know of anyone who did so voluntarily, although I do know some whose trip home was involuntary.

But knowing we could be sent home for infractions didn't, of course, stop me or anyone else from breaking the rules. My infractions were relatively mild, to include several illegal plane rides.

Just before I left Danang I went up in a Bird Dog, those little planes with two seats. I knew a guy who flew one, so I asked him to take me up and he did.

His assignment was to check out possible mortar or rocket sites near Hoi An. So we went down and looked at them. He decided they should be destroyed so he called in artillery and also shot four rockets from the plane. The rockets scared me to death—it felt like the plane was going to fall apart. When it got dark, he told me if I saw flashes on the ground to let him know because that could mean we were getting shot at. That too made me wonder what I was doing up there.

I went on an illegal day-trip to Hue in December [1967] just to see the city (as I reported in a letter home). "It was strictly illegal, of course, because it's off limits, but we knew a pilot who flew up there in an Otter that he let me fly back, or steer, which is really cool.

At Hue he found somebody there who could drive me around the city, and we drove around for about two hours and saw the old capital and university. I glad I went because it's the one nice town that I've ever seen in Vietnam."

Another illegal trip was just a stop-off to see a Donut Dollie friend at Phu Loi when I was coming back to Cu Chi from R&R. I planned to stay overnight, but I hadn't planned on a new Donut Dollie honcho being there who could turn me in. Fortunately she didn't. When I went to the airstrip to hitch a ride back to Cu Chi the next day, it was difficult to persuade the controllers not to broadcast that a Donut Dollie was looking for a ride, in case Saigon, dreaded Saigon, was listening.

In October I flew out to two Special Force camps with another girl. She knew an SF guy very well—in fact she would have married him had he not been killed the year before. This was the camp where they had dedicated a dispensary to him because he was a medic and he had set it up.

I'm still envious of the girl who got to fly in an F4 with a pilot she was dating. I never thought to ask a chopper pilot if I could do the cyclical, although learning to fly a helicopter has been on my bucket list ever since. When I told a chopper pilot years later at the Wall that all I wanted to do was hover, he laughed at my ignorance of not knowing that was the hardest maneuver of all.

Letter. Oct. 1, Danang

One really fun thing we did recently was go to a movie after work at a movie theatre in the same area where we work. The fun part was afterwards when we were given a ride in a helicopter most of the way home because one of the girls had come in one. It was strictly illegal because we aren't supposed to fly after dark, especially on unauthorized business, but since the head honcho was with us we really couldn't get into too much trouble.

All of us went to a party at Cu Chi where there was music and lots of dancing. We were having a great time but curfew was rapidly approaching. Our rather strict Unit Director was with us. What to do.

"Let's turn our watches back."

"She'll never fall for it."

"Let's try it anyway."

And so we did, getting all the men to turn their watches back too, just by half an hour and then since that worked so well, another half hour until we decided we'd pushed our luck far enough and had to call it a night.

This is one of the best Rule Breaking experiences I've heard so far, done with the knowledge, if not approval, of the Red Cross powers-that-be. Donut Dollies could not be married, but after Vietnam many did marry men they met during their tour. Kit Sparrow Cotton tells her story.

I met my husband John at my first assignment in Tuy Hoa. We had arrived in country the same day. He was a dashing fighter pilot, and I was about as green and naive as they come. He followed me all over country, going up into the tower at Tuy Hoa, asking if any chopper pilot would like to give a fighter pilot a lift to Camp Enari (Pleiku) or Cam Ranh Army. Many times when I turned around, there he was!

Before getting married, we wanted to travel around the world before returning to the "real world." However, my father said in his "General's Voice," "No daughter of MINE is going to travel around the world with a man to whom she is not wed!" So, in a way, he forced our hands. It took much paperwork and several trips to Saigon to qualify for a Vietnamese wedding. And each time we thought we were getting married, only to return to our bases as singles. One time, in order to be married in a certain councilman's district, we had to post our intentions on telephone poles in his area so that if anyone had any objections, he could voice them with the councilman. We must have looked funny—a pin-striped gal and a khaki-clad man hammering up papers on any pole we could find!

Finally, FINALLY the day came. Romantique Rosanna (Sturtevant), another DD who ended up being my maid of honor, and a friend of John's joined us around a red and white checkered oil-cloth-covered table where we jokingly wondered if this would be the location of our marriage ceremony. Suddenly, two huge wooden doors swung open, and we were ushered into the councilman's office where the solemn Vietnamese councilman sat dressed to the nines with a sash across his chest. The walls were lined with wooden bookcases, and the joking air a few minutes earlier suddenly turned somber. This was it! We were finally going to become Capt and Mrs. John Cotton.

The ceremony was conducted in Vietnamese/French (I am fluent in that language), the words of union were spoken, and in Vietnamese we were pronounced man and wife. Immediately afterwards we went to RC HQ where I turned in my Red Cross status (but just for one brief moment I WAS a married DD), and I fell under the umbrella of the US Air Force protection. A couple days later we left on our honeymoon which was cut short in India where John got hepatitis from eating shellfish that must have been caught in the Ganges.

We had a religious ceremony in Japan at a base chapel because John's brother was stationed there, and then we went back to Ft. Myer, VA, where my parents had a "propah" reception for us. Shortly thereafter we left for Lakenheath, England, our first assignment which lasted four years.

And here we are 46 and a half years later—still husband and wife with three children and nine grands. What an adventure this life has been! And to think we owe it all to Clara and the Red Cross!

Parties!!!

20

"I don't want to go."

"But you have to go. We've been invited."

"I don't care. I'm not going!"

My best friend, Loretta, and I were having a strong disagreement at the weekly staff meeting in Danang. We Donut Dollies were frequently invited to parties—promotion parties, ETS [Estimated Time of Separation, i.e., going home] parties, stand downs, we-got-entertainment parties, we-just-got-a-shipment-of-steak parties, party parties.

Our response to these invitations varied between, "I don't have to go if I don't want to" to "We have to go to all of them." I fell in the latter extreme, as did most of the other girls.

I learned you can eat four steak dinners in an evening. The units would invite us to share cook-outs with them when they got steaks, and one evening at Cu Chi all the units must have gotten a shipment because we had four invitations for dinner. Not wanting to let anyone down, I and a couple of other girls made the rounds. Since I knew I wouldn't be able to eat four full meals, I held back on everything but the steak so that I could oohh and aahh as I chewed those four tough, grisly, cooked-to-within-an-inch-of-becoming-leather steaks—all while exclaiming about how wonderful it was.

War is hell.

Letter. May 2, An Khe

Last night four of us Donut Dollies ate at the officers' mess, i.e., big-wigs and a 1-star general. The officers were nice and fun; the general is a little scary just because he's a general, but we got into a joking fight about the merits of Colorado (he didn't like it, unbelievable as it seems). I defended it, of course, and he became human.

We are invited to tons of parties, but they're usually officers' parties, and although some of them are nice, the EMs have convinced me that lifers are bad sorts. However, to be fair, some are very fun—it's just that even at parties we're still on parade and can't say anything sharp because we're Red Cross girls. However, that doesn't always stop me.

Letter. May 22, An Khe

I've just gotten back from an officers' party which at first seemed like it was going to be one of the typical ones where the officers get really drunk and make fools of themselves with the girls. Granted, there were a lot of officers like that there, but there was one Warrant Officer, i.e., person trained for special duty—in the case of the 1st Cav usually as a pilot—who was really fun to talk to. We talked about various things—our backgrounds, friends, etc., and it was on more than a superficial level. That's one of the things we really crave.

I find I don't have much in common with lifers (men who are in the military as a career) because their lives are mapped out for them according to rules and regulations.

I guess that is why I like the EMs best (among other reasons— same age, interests, the fact that we have the most contact with them), but also because the army isn't their life. They have other interests which they live for.

Letter. June 23, An Khe

I went to a party of a group of guys I had met at Phan Thiet who had all sorts of spirit and cohesiveness throughout the whole brigade. I was the only girl and they were singing brigade songs from song sheets. It was really incredible to see grown men acting like that—really gave me a good feeling. I've been to several other parties recently—some good, some bad. Often the men are drunk, and it just depends on how they act when they're drunk—often not too good!

Letter. Aug. 28, Danang

Life here is definitely more exciting in some ways in that we see more shows, etc. I've seen lots of USO shows, some of which are really good. Also had dinner with Robert Stack, alias Elliot Ness on TV. He was just going around into the field seeing the guys for somewhat the same reasons we do—he came because these guys are here for good or bad and he wants to do what he can to make them a little happier. Also last night we saw the Miss America with the Miss America of 1966 and about 6 of the other girls. They were really cute girls, altho not raving beauties. They put on a show of songs which I enjoyed but some that the guys weren't too excited about. For instance, they sang a song about college football which the guys really couldn't associate with.

Tape. Dec., Cu Chi

Every Sunday we go over and eat dinner in the General's mess which is pretty nice, but it kind of makes me nervous talking to all those head honchos. We saw a movie afterwards, and then everyone left and all that were left were the guys who wait on tables and mind the bar. There were four of them and they were talking about all the majors and colonels and captains. The girls see the officers in an entirely different light than the guys, and the guys have the real story on it. They see them when they're not just putting on an act for the girls. It was fun to hear all the gossip about them.

Tape. Feb. 11, Cu Chi

I went to a going-away party in division headquarters where there were people like majors and colonels and also the two-star general, the commanding general of the division. He is a very severe type, short grey hair, very nice but also very stately. I couldn't believe it but this guy got up and was doing his version of the frug or rock and roll with one of the girls. The two-star general up there bopping around!

Propositions

21

I didn't write home about being propositioned, but I had plenty to say about it in emails later, and we DDs often talk about that aspect of our year of living with and around hundreds of men. I think the response I like best that one DD told me about was just to laugh at the suggestion.

Just like everything else, a story needs sex and violence to sell. Hey, we got all that.

Death is a given. Sex? How about the morning, during a spell when the rumor was going around that the girls put out for money and some were getting propositioned, a guy came up to me in the Red Cross center at An Khe, my first assignment, and asked if he could ask me a personal question. I thought, "Oh, great, 8:30 in the morning and I'm going to get my first proposition." I hesitantly said yes, and he shyly said, "Where are you from?"

Intrigue (and sex and death)? Would the F4 pilot get back from his flight for his date with a DD that night? Answer...no. Would the guys we just played that silly game with before they were airlifted out on a mission get hit? Answer...yes.

Yeah, we had it all.

We were invited to share the relaxation time when the men came in from the field for their stand downs. One time at Cu Chi it went too far. There was a Filipino band playing old favorites like "Proud Mary" and "We Gotta Get Out of This Place," and then a comedian telling jokes we didn't want to hear. Things were getting rowdy when our officer escorts said we should leave. As they escorted us away, drunk men came up to us making suggestive comments. That was the only time in Vietnam that I felt the least bit of fear being surrounded by hundreds of men, and it was our own fault for staying too long. And it was the only time I can remember that anyone said or did anything inappropriate, except for the Marine officer who pinched me going in the officers' club at Danang. I was not pleased!

I have a great photo of girls programming in an EM club with a huge picture of a naked reclining woman above the bar behind the girls. No wonder the guys sometimes got "confused" about our role!

DD programming in an EM club at Cu Chi with pin-up on wall

At Cu Chi there was a girl from Ireland who was selling cars to the guys for when they got back to the States. She went to the parties with us...and came home with us. A few times guys told me they thought she was doing it for money. I said, well, she goes to and comes back from the parties with us, so if you're accusing her, you're accusing us. All the women there were fair game for speculation.

My take on these fantasy stories and "remembrances" of the guys is this. They were young men in a combat zone who had very little to think about except Jody [the guy back home who was stealing his girl], fear, death and girls—and Donut Dollies were the closest round-eyes they could see. Boys will be boys, and when they remember their youth, they are still boys. These stupid and sometimes insulting memories are just that—memories from grown men trying to recapture their youth, still acting and thinking like boys.

I don't say that to denigrate or excuse them. The part that hurts, though, is that we know they thought some of these hurtful things then, and some still do now. Many of us have felt that hurt, which feels like a stark betrayal. The pain they caused and may still cause is their responsibility. We can hold our heads high and feel pride in what we did. They know it too, as many of us have heard when we've been thanked by veterans at the Wall.

Tet!!

22

Tet was when the country blew up—north and south, in cities and villages, at main base camps, LZs and firebases. Charlie (VC and NVA) seemed to be everywhere, and nowhere was safe.

Tape. Jan. 30, Cu Chi

We're in a big tense moment now because it's Tet, the Vietnamese holiday, and one of the army posts not too far from here was infiltrated the other day and an officers' club was blown up, so they've been really strict about people not congregating at clubs. The clubs are closed at 8:00 and some of the guys have been restricted to their quarters or office at 8:00, which is a complete drag. And this might go on for four more days. It's been going on for three days now, but I guess I can suffer through. It's a pain in the neck though because we can't go out to see the men.

The 25th Division has been getting into lots of trouble. They have been getting a lot of body count, but they have been getting a lot of guys hurt too. Choppers have been going down. It's a pretty tense time, but we're doing well. There is a lot of action down here. It's more than I thought there was. Maybe it's just that I know more about it. I seem to be a lot more aware of the war here than I was in An Khe, although I might have if I'd stayed there longer. As a matter of fact, I miss An Khe an awful lot. I'm trying to get sent up there TDY. I think there are a lot of things here that I wouldn't have had in An Khe.

I hear from various reports that the Cav is going north, way up north where the Marines are, which is interesting. I don't know what they're going to do with the girls and all, but I hope I get sent up there before too long while they're still in An Khe and I get to see what's happening up there. I'm trying to go out to the field here,

117

but the 25th Division is just impossible. They just won't let us go out. I get a feeling of real frustration, but there are other things to make up for it, thank goodness. We go to EM clubs a lot in the evening. It's fun to see them after hours and have interesting talks with them.

Tape. Feb. 11, Cu Chi

I guess I ought to tell you what has been happening here, all the mess that has been happening on Tet, that is the Vietnamese New Year. It all started the 29th. I don't know how much they have been telling you about it. I'm sure you've heard all the mess in Saigon and everything, but I don't know how much you have heard about Cu Chi. They went through a pretty tense period for about five days when Saigon was getting hit and we were being mortared and rocketed. We spent quite a few nights in the bunker—sleeping in the bunker which is a novel experience sleeping four or five people in a bunker—but it has pretty much calmed down here now, although there is still some action in Saigon. We still get a few mortar attacks but we are used to them. After the first night—the first night was really scary because we were getting rocketed then—but since then it has been pretty good. People's nerves are pretty much on edge, though, because almost everybody is sleeping in bunkers because there is lots of artillery. In fact you will probably hear some of that as I'm taping. Sometimes we don't know whether it's outgoing or incoming. But it's okay. There, did you hear that?

Our Red Cross honchos in Saigon asked if we wanted to leave to go to Saigon, but we all said no. One girl got sort of panicky when the rockets started and was crying, but mostly we toughed it out okay.

One of the girls will be transferred here after all the big action stops. She's been stuck in Saigon during all the mess. She had been transferred out here and she left about two or three days later because the artillery made her so nervous, but we are kind of used to it so it's not so bad. She'll be coming back when it all calms down though.

It has been really interesting, this whole big business because the Viet Cong are making such a strong move. It has me convinced that when they want to, they can really go pretty far, much farther than we give them credit for because we used to have at least half of the 25th Division force out on the two forward base camps, but since all this mess, we have moved everything back. There used to be one or two artillery units here. Now there are five. I heard Cu Chi and all of our infantry units are around Cu Chi or in Saigon, and it has moved the whole action of the war for the 25th Division away from the Cambodian border down to Saigon. It means that although we thought we cleared Charlie out from this area, when he wants to he can come back. I don't know how long he can keep up this big push. I guess it's going on in the north as well as here. I guess the main centers are Saigon and the DMZ. I don't know how active it is in the other places, but if he can push this hard here, I really wonder how far he could get if he really really wanted to. Of course, the thing that is hard to determine is how long he can keep it up, how many supplies he has and how much ammunition he has, but from various reports, captured guys have pretty good weapons and they aren't skinny and stuff like that. So it is all a big puzzle and nobody knows what is going to happen or at least nobody tells us or seems to know what is happening with the war right now. All we know is Charlie is on the move and we don't know how far he will go.

Letter. Mid-Feb., Cu Chi

This war is making me sicker and sicker. The 25th Division is getting smashed. We can't take Charlie's position and we just keep going in and getting more and more casualties. One company in the Wolfhounds is down to one officer in the whole company—there should be six, and there just aren't enough to replace all the officers who are getting killed or wounded. A young Negro sergeant I knew in the Wolfhounds was killed yesterday—a really nice funny guy. And there's no end in sight. When I come home I just want to forget about the war. I don't even want to read newspapers about it. It's too upsetting to hear about it and know what they're going through and not be able to help in any way. I thought I was getting hardened, but when I think of those guys out there now, and then knowing they're in the worst fighting they've ever seen with no respite, it makes me sick for them. It would take a heck of a lot to justify this war with all the suffering of the guys here and their families at home.

I felt very slightly for the first time last night what it must be like for guys in the field never being able to sleep peacefully, always wondering where Charlie is, knowing the next day your chances of getting killed or at least wounded are pretty good and then seeing your buddies getting hurt. I know I've said all this before, but like I said, I felt it last night and it makes it much more real.

Tape. Feb. 28, Cu Chi

We have been getting attacks every third night or so. Last night I slept in the bunker because we had one and I just couldn't face going back out three or four times during the night. You asked about that artillery, the noises that were in the background of my last tape. That's artillery that's outgoing. The guns are about a mile from here, but it sounds pretty loud. Actually, since I was in the bunker, the sound is muffled. The sound is much louder than that. But firing like that doesn't happen very often during the day. It's outgoing fire. It's not rifles or anything like that or mortars coming in.

I was at a club last night that lots of the 5th Mech Infantry, mechanized infantry, come to—guys that come in because they're hurt or something. I was talking with one of the guys in one of the companies who has been fighting down by Saigon. He said that they've had 65% casualties in the 3/4 Cav, which is a tank battalion, and this company, Charlie Company, that he was from has 32 guys left out of a company of about 150. It's really incredible what's happening down in Saigon. We're getting completely chewed up. Nobody can believe what's happening. They just relieved the 2nd Brigade Commander who has been the commander only about 3 weeks. He is the one that's in charge of all the troops down there and he just got relieved. It is really a messed up situation.

I don't know if I'll come right home when I leave or what. Right now I just feel like coming home and relaxing and not worrying about anything. But also I'd like to go back to Australia, away from war news, riots, strikes, politics, etc., etc., all of which make me sick.

Enough, enough.

Even though I was at Cu Chi during Tet and spent a lot of time in our bunker and several days filling sandbags to reinforce it, I still love fireworks. Mortars were bad enough and when the rockets started with their whistling it was even scarier, but I even like the whistling fireworks. I know it sounds weird, but some of my favorite memories are during that time.

There was a group of guys that lived on the edge of the airstrip who I would go visit after mortar attacks. One day I saw two of my favorite guys walking toward me and when they saw me, they started limping and hanging onto each other—for sympathy—and laughing. One had in fact been hurt and had a bandage on his head.

My buddies who lived near the airstrip in good health

When the mortars started at night, there were two of us who would be running out the doors hollering "in-coming" practically before the mortars hit. We were finely tuned to recognize the difference between out-going and in-coming in our sleep. And then one night Charlie blew up headquarters which was right next door to our hooch. No one was hurt.

I was recording messages home to my parents during that time, and for some reason I would record the out-going mortars at the beginning of the tape so they could hear it. This was near the end of my tour and I think I was kind of immune to the effect it might have on them.

When I went back in '93, we were renovating a clinic at Cu Chi with Vietnamese veterans. As we came to know them, I learned that one of them was head of munitions at Cu Chi during Tet—in effect, the man who was throwing mortars at me.

We Gotta Get Out
of This Place

23

I was only slightly over half my year tour when I wrote this letter shortly after being transferred from Danang to Cu Chi.

Letter. Nov., Cu Chi

I'm getting a desperate feeling that I'm leaving too soon and I have to see all the people I can while I can. I dreamed last night that I was home again and had been for a few days and I woke up crying because I missed it here so much—real live tears. It's going to really hurt. I can't imagine what it will be like to have it all over with forever. I get very sad when I think about it.

Last tape. April, Cu Chi

One of the pilots I had known when I was up in Danang got shot down. Another pilot that I had talked to the night before got shot down the next day. And a guy I knew down here got killed in a mortar attack—a lieutenant. The longer I stay, the more people I hear about getting killed.

When I'm packing I keep thinking of all these things that I want to tell you about and the story behind them, but right now I'm just tired and I'm ready to leave, I guess. Like I said, I'm not really sad but I think that deep down inside there is just sort of—I don't know. I know it's time to go, and I know...., and it's sad. Right now, all I want to do is come straight home and have it be spring and have you be there and sleep and see friends and go swimming and drive a car and try to forget about this. I better go before I get really depressed, but I'll see you soon. Bye.

My departure from Vietnam was delayed because Tan San Nhut [the airport in Saigon] was taking mortar fire. While waiting for the mortaring to die down, I befriended an Air Force F4 pilot and his sergeant who were derosing at the same time. They had a spray can of red paint and a small stencil of a phantom—big hat, cape billowing behind. They were going around the airport spraying various places that needed a phantom stencil, which was anything that didn't move. Then we decided to branch out to things that moved. They thought I needed one on the shoulder of my uniform, to which I agreed. I suggested the officer get one on his khaki uniform, to which he eventually succumbed as well. When we boarded the Braniff plane, we asked the stewardess if she wanted one too. She laughingly declined, but did allow as to how the plane could use one by the door, so we obliged.

When we took off, it was fast and steep. Nobody breathed until the captain came on the intercom and announced that we were at 2000 feet. There was a slight cheer and we were safely on our way. The major and I sat together and talked most of the way across the Pacific until we got to Travis AFB where we parted to find whatever flight we could to continue on home.

As a strange follow-up.... I stopped off in Denver on my way home to go to the wedding of a DD and a man she'd met at Cu Chi. A few days later, when I boarded the plane to take me on home to NJ, who should be on the plane but the phantom sprayer. I put my hand on his arm, he looked at me, another passenger saw the look and quickly offered his seat so we could sit together to continue our conversation.

I like to think there's still a plane flying around with a little phantom on its entryway.

Short-Timer's Letters

24

The short-timer's letters were sent back to the States to forewarn friends and relatives about what to expect and how to act around their home-coming GI. We distributed them and then made up our own for ourselves.

For the Men

Dear Civilians, Friends, Draft Dodgers, etc.:

In the near future the undersigned will be once more in your midst, dehydrated and demoralized, to take his place again as a human being, with the well-known forms of freedom and justice for all; to engage in life, liberty, and the somewhat delayed pursuit of happiness. In making your joyous preparations to welcome him back into organized society you should provide certain allowances to the crude environment which has been his miserable lot for the past twelve months. In other words, he might be a little Asiatic from Vietnamesis and overseasitis, and should be handled with care. Do not be alarmed if he is infected with all forms of rare tropical diseases. A little time in the land of the Big PX will cure that malady.

Therefore, show no alarm if he insists on carrying a weapon to the dinner table, looks around for his steel pot when offered a seat, or wakes you up in the middle of the night for guard duty. Keep cool when he pours gravy on his dessert or mixes peaches with his Seagram's VO. Pretend not to notice if he eats with his fingers instead of silverware and prefers C-rats to steak. Take it with a smile when he insists on digging up the garden to fill sandbags for the bunker he is building. Be tolerant when he takes his blanket and sheet off the bed and puts them on the floor to sleep.

Abstain from saying anything about powdered eggs, dehydrated potatoes, fried rice, fresh milk or ice cream. Do not be alarmed if he should jump up from the dinner table and rush to the garbage can to wash his dish with a toilet brush. After all, this has been his standard. Also, if it should start raining, pay no attention to him if he pulls off his clothes, grabs a bar of soap and towel, and runs outdoors for a shower.

When in his daily conversation he utters such things as: "xin loi" and "choi oi" just be patient, and simply leave quickly and calmly if by some chance he utters "didi" with an irritated look on his face, because it means no less than "get the H___ out of here." Do not let it shake you up if he picks up the phone and yells "Parchment Sir" or says "Roger out" for good-bye, or simply "working."

Never ask why the Jones' son had a higher rank than he did, and by no means mention the term "extend." Pretend not to notice if at a restaurant he calls the waitress "number one girl" and uses his hat for an ashtray. He will probably keep listening for "Homeward Bound" or "Coming Home Soldier" to sound off over AFRS. If he does, comfort him, for he is still reminiscing. Be especially watchful when he is in the presence of a woman———especially a beautiful one.

Above all, keep in mind that beneath that tanned and rugged exterior there is a heart of gold (the only thing of value he has left). Treat him with kindness, tolerance, and an occasional 5th of good liquor, and you will be able to rehabilitate that which was once (and now is a hollow shell of) the happy-go-lucky guy you once knew and loved. Last, but by no means least, send no more mail to the APO, fill the ice box with beer, get the civvies out of mothballs, fill the car with gas, and get the women and children off the roads....

BECAUSE THE KID IS COMING HOME ! ! ! ! ! ! ! !

_____
Signature

For the Donut Dollies

Dear Civilians, Friends, Draft Dodgers, Glamour Girls, Etc.,

In the very near future the undersigned will be once more in your midst, dehydrated and demoralized to take her place again as a human-being, with the well-known forms of freedom and justice for all: to engage in life, liberty and the somewhat delayed pursuit of happiness. In making your joyous preparations to welcome her back into organized society you should provide certain allowance for the crude environment which has been her miserable lot for the past twelve months. In other words, she might be a little Asiatic from Vietnamenitis and oversensitive and should be handled with care. Do not be alarmed if she is infested with all forms of rare tropical diseases. A little time in the "Land of the Big PX" will cure the malady.

Therefore, show no alarm if she rushes to the dining room to be the first one served, stops men on the street to ask where they are from, drops her clothes on the floor and lets them lay, and never makes her bed except in extreme emergencies. Pretend not to notice if she eats with her fingers and eats lunchmeat instead of steak. Keep cool when she pours gravy on her dessert or mixes peaches with her Seagrams VO. Think nothing of it when a car backfires and she yells "Incoming" and dives under the bed.

Do not be surprised if in a group of people she immediately takes charge, divides them into two teams and starts playing games. DO NOT offer to introduce her to any new young men—especially if they are in the military. Abstain from mentioning powdered eggs, dehydrated potatoes, fried rice and recombined milk and ice cream.

Do not be upset if when walking down the street she stops and stares at other women, especially their clothes or hairdos. There is a scarcity of the female "round eyes" in Nam. When in her daily conversation she utters such things as "xin loi," and "shei si" just be patient. Leave quickly and calmly if by some chance she utters "DIDI" with an irritate look on her face, because it means no less than "get the h—- out of here." Do not let it shake you up if she picks up the phone and yells, "Parchment, sir" or simply shouts "WORKING."

When you go shopping, do not get too embarrassed when she asks the clerk for the price of something and no matter what it is she will argue, scream and yell, "you beaucoup Dinky Dau" and try to get him to lower the price. Explain to her nicely that you must pay what the man asks. Do not criticize her in a restaurant or any public place if she immediately strikes up a conversation with the nearest male. This has been her job for 12 months.

Understand that she is not always happy. The smile was been worn for 12 months and is a hard habit to break. Don't ever give her a direct order! She has been a civilian amongst many military and she was spoiled by them. No one gave her a direct order and she refuses to acknowledge one now.

If you find something missing, do not accuse her stealing, just go into her room and retrieve the items. She is so used to scrounging items and getting a back-log for trading she will continue for some time. Be patient. When she goes shopping, do not be upset when she returns with 5 cans of hairspray, 20 bars of soap, 15 cans of baby powder and a case of laundry soap. She is used to getting these items in large quantities when they are available.

When she goes on her first American date, be discreet and say nothing about the way she enters and leaves the car. As they were a scarcity in Nam she is used to climbing in, on, and even to seat herself. She'll learn to be ladylike if given time.

For a while after returning home do not mention card games to her; namely hearts, rummy, pinochle, or back alley bridge. If she doesn't screech and pull her hair out upon hearing this, she will inevitably sit you down for 4 or 5 hours and beat the pants off you.

If going to visit a friend in the hospital, leave her behind or be prepared to have her go up and down the halls visiting all of the patients before you can leave. Do not offer her coffee or kool-aid as she might say something wrong. Her language may be a bit salty after her sojourn in the military.

Don't ever give her a light blue dress for a present. She may burn, tear or simply ignore it. Refrain from inviting her to any parties where she must think up an idea to play games. You may regret your invitation.

When it starts raining, do not be alarmed to see her pulling out a green poncho and putting on knee high boots. She is conditioned to the monsoon season. Just sit and wait patiently for the rain to stop.

And, by NO means, ask her what did she do in Vietnam?!!

Above all, keep in mind that beneath that tanned, blue-covered exterior beats a heart of pure gold (the only thing of value she has left). Treat her with kindness, tolerance and an occasional 5th of good liquor, and you will be able to rehabilitate that which was once (and now is) a hollow shell of the happy-go-lucky girl you once knew and loved.

Last, but by no means least, send no more mail to the APO, fill the ice box with beer, get the civvies out of the mothballs, fill the car with gas, and get the men and children off the streets.....

BECAUSE THE DONUT DOLLIE IS COMING HOME!!!!!!!!!!!!!!!!!!!

_____

Signature

Part II

The Aftermath

My Brother

25

Three months after I got back from Vietnam, my brother went over as a Marine lieutenant with Kilo 3/7. He was killed three weeks later on July 28, 1968. Words can't express the ongoing tragedy of that.

A soft summer night

It was a warm summer night. The fireflies were just beginning to come out. Mother was getting the barbeque ready to cook dinner. Daddy was going to be out of town for a few days, leaving directly from the office, but there would be several of us for dinner. My older brother was living in town for the summer with his wife and 2-year-old son. A Red Cross friend of mine was visiting before we set out on a cross-country trip in my brand new Mustang convertible, my welcome home present to myself.

Unexpectedly the front door opened and Daddy walked in. I saw the stunned look on his face and thought, "Tell me he's been wounded. Please say he's only been wounded."

Going in circles

They came from all over, but mostly from up and down the east coast. The word spread, like wildfire—I don't know how. And they gathered at our house the night before the memorial service. Mostly his college friends, but others as well. One young man appeared at our front door, and Mother asked, confused, "Who are you?" He said, "Colemy"—Bill Coleman from our childhood days of hide-and-seek. He'd heard and come.

We, the "young" ones, stayed downstairs that night, telling stories about him. All I remember is stories with laughter. Later Mother told me my grandmother, disturbed, asked, why are they laughing, and Mother tried to explain.

The next day, the day of the service, one of his three best college friends who was to give the eulogy was sick, couldn't get out of bed. Mother went to his room, put her cool hands on his forehead as she had done for all of us children throughout our childhoods, and talked to him.

He got up, put on his Marine uniform, went to the church and told us about Billy, his friend. It took 25 more years for him to talk with us about Billy and Vietnam again, although we heard from him or saw him yearly, usually in July. And then, finally, he told us that Billy had asked him to "look out for my sister and mother, the others will be okay, but I'm worried about them."

Then, several weeks later his body came home. We had a quiet funeral, and I called the good friends of my parents and mine who were spending part of the summer on Long Island to ask if I could come visit. I needed to get away. Billy's Marine college friend drove me out there.

As we drove through a country intersection, he couldn't make up his mind which way to go, so he drove in a complete circle around it. I laughed, and wondered about this serious, sad guy who would drive in circles in the middle of nowhere.

I don't like to tell people that my brother was killed in Vietnam, and I rarely do. People that knew him understand the magnitude of the loss, so I don't have to tell them. I don't like to tell the general public, even friends, because they just don't understand Vietnam. And I can see them thinking, "Oh, now I understand why Nancy's so hung up on Vietnam," as if his death explains it all away. I see my experience and his as almost completely separate and very different. I had gone and come back before he went over. Mine was positive in many ways, his was all negative.

I sometimes tell veterans, usually for a specific reason as it pertains to a conversation or situation, but I don't like to tell them because it only adds to their already too-heavy burden. You might think talking to other families, particularly siblings, would be the easiest, when in fact it's the hardest. It's the hardest not because I empathize so much with them, but rather so little—my feelings shut down with siblings, especially sisters.

But the real reason I don't tell people is because no matter how close they are to me or my family or to Billy, no matter how deeply they believe or know what a wonderful person he was, no matter how hard they try or want to empathize, they can't understand the enormity of the loss. Now I know intellectually that this isn't always true, but that's how it feels. I know, intellectually, he would want me to share him with others, and to let him go.

Jonathan Shay, author of *Achilles in Vietnam* and *Odysseus in America*, wrote something a while ago which I had heard before, but which seems to have hit home recently. He said, "Persistence of guilt, rage, and grief are often assertions that there is at least one person who still cares about justice, that someone is keeping faith with the dead, that someone is asserting meaning in the face of events for which meaning could not be found."

I think many of us, in our grieving, become walking memorials to our lost buddy, brother. In our grief, people who were unable or unwilling to express their condolences can witness the effects of our loss and their own inadequacy. This becomes particularly effective if you don't tell people you're grieving or resentful or angry or needy because then they can't possibly make restitution or reach the part of you that needs the response.

The reason I'm writing this to you all is that I think it may be possible to lessen my grief by sharing it with a community of veterans that can understand, in their own way, and who are willing to take on some of that grief with me. I think again about the Wailing Wall article I mentioned in an earlier post [Bearing Witness—see VWAR chapter]. It was about the traditional ceremonies which the Jewish community participates in at regular intervals throughout the year to commemorate and remember losses. Because of this sharing and recognition, the victims are not isolated in their grief and so are better able to integrate it into their lives.

So I'm taking this step of telling you that, yes, my younger brother, Billy, was killed in Vietnam, he was a wonderful person, and I miss him.

When I saw the movie *Taking Chance*, I teared up at the first scene and continued on through much of it— mostly when they had scenes of the respect that everyone showed to Chance and his escort. I don't remember much about when my brother died because I was in such a pain-filled fog. One thing I do remember

Billy playing soccer at Dartmouth College

is at the memorial service sitting next to the Marine escorts and thinking how hard it must be for them to have this duty, seeing the pain of a family member first-hand.

Several years ago I learned that a man who was in Billy's actual ambush lived here in Fairbanks. We got together and he told me about it in great detail which was both good and bad.

He's from Hawaii and his wife had a hula dance studio, so from time to time I would see them performing at events where he'd be wearing his Hawaiian shirt playing the ukulele. It was surreal to think that this was a man who had been one of the last people to see my brother.

Billy and me at his OCS graduation from Quantico

Dreams of My Brother

26

The dreams I have about my brother Billy occur only every several years but there is a strange similarity to them. I describe them in these emails to the email group Brothers and Sisters In Touch.

2005.

I had another one of those dreams—one of the ones I have every year or so about my brother—my younger brother—for some reason I think it's important to say that. As in all my dreams about my brother, there's always a split. I always know he's either dead and alive at the same time, or he's alive but I know he's going to die. In this one, he was going to die—I knew it, but he didn't.

The only part I really remember is that we had a long quiet hug—just a hug. He was big, strong, like in the pictures I see of him—although I don't remember it in reality—with a big thick neck. That Marine leatherneck, I guess. But he was big, like my protector, of me, the older sister.

I think that in the dream I knew it was a dream, but I wanted to hold onto it. I had him again for a moment, even though I knew it had a sad ending.

I dream about him only about once a year and I usually don't know what sparks it. And in the morning, I'm not sure if I'm glad I had it or would rather not. I wonder if these dreams are a poor attempt to fill in the huge gap I have of missing him....

2006.

I had a dream about Billy a week or so ago. As is always the case in my dreams about him he's alive in the dream but he's either also dead or I know he's going to die. We were at a family gathering and he'd told me earlier that he'd just gotten orders to go back to Iraq the next morning. He hadn't told the rest of the family and didn't go downstairs to the gathering because he needed to prepare himself—not physically but mentally. Throughout the dream, I knew he was going to die. As the word spread among the family, I woke up. It just makes me so sad to still be missing him so much.

I *don't remember the dream but this is what I wrote about it:* In fact, in real life, my brother had gone into the Red Cross recreation center in Danang and asked if any of the girls knew me. (He went to Vietnam three months after I got back.) By the time the word got to Jackie who was in the back office, he had already gone. I've always regretted that she didn't talk to him so he could do more than just look at what I did over there, and so she could tell me about him.

As with all these dreams, it leaves me sad that I have to make up stories about him instead of having him in real life.

Back in the World

27

The World, the Land of the Big PX, home—the place where life would return to normal. The men would get that good job, buy that hot car, marry their girl, and live happily ever after. But, of course, often it wasn't to be. We women had some similar and some different experiences adjusting back to "normal" life.

In these emails written at different time periods, I tell about what I did to deal with being back in the World, a struggle that continues to this day.

Coming home was very strange. My very special younger brother went over there as a Marine lieutenant three months after I got back and was killed three weeks later. Several months after that I went back into the Red Cross and worked in recreation in military hospitals at Fort Knox, Kentucky, and Jacksonville, Florida. That provided me a place to still be with my guys and come down somewhat from the war. It didn't, however, give me a place to grieve.

I have ached for the men and for the women, and I guess subliminally for myself, ever since. I have been unable to leave the war and my experience. I've worked as a volunteer at the Wall since it was built and worked with other programs to assist families and veterans. I also organize a Stand Down and have been a counselor at the Vet Center here in Fairbanks.

Three months after I got back from Vietnam, my brother went over as a Marine lieutenant. He was killed three weeks later on July 28, 1968. I then went back to work for the Red Cross as a recreation worker at Ft. Knox, Kentucky, for about 15 months.

For eight years during the 90's, after 20 years of approach/avoidance, I spent several winter months of each year in Washington, DC, "doing" Vietnam. I've been a Park Service volunteer at the Wall since two months after it was dedicated, so during my time in DC I spent several days there, plus one day a week at the warehouse where the items that are left at the Wall are taken. The main thing I did was work on the In Touch program with the Friends of the Vietnam Veterans Memorial—a program that connected families who lost someone in Vietnam with veterans who knew that person.

Following the lead of many people who came before me for the challenge, adventure and lure of Alaska, I've lived in Fairbanks, Alaska since 1972.

At age 50, after 20+ years of doing temporary secretarial work at the University of Alaska (I couldn't find a career, especially one that held the excitement of Vietnam, and besides, this gave me freedom to travel), I went back to school for a Master's degree in Community Psychology. For eleven years I then worked two days a week as a volunteer counselor at the Vet Center.

I went back to Vietnam in 1993 with the Veterans Vietnam Restoration Project, working for two weeks with Vietnamese veterans to renovate a clinic at Cu Chi (where I'd been stationed during Tet) and then traveling for two weeks throughout the country. A very difficult but healing trip.

For years and years I struggled with what to do with Vietnam. I volunteered at the Vet Center for a few months, took counseling courses with the idea of using them with vets, let it all go for several years, started volunteering at the Wall in 1983 for a few days at a time when I was in the east—but I kept feeling like I needed/wanted to do more. I told a few people about having been to Vietnam but reluctantly because of the strange reactions I'd get. (One woman who'd known me for about 10 years came up to me one day and said she'd just heard that I was a helicopter pilot in Vietnam. Other friends and I got a good laugh out of that—now they refer to me as "Nancy the door-gunner.")

So the struggle continued until I finally said to myself, "JUST DO IT." I decided to go to Washington in 1990 and immerse myself in Vietnam for several months at a time, which I continued to do for eight years. I worked at the Wall and for the Friends of the Vietnam Veterans Memorial and talked about Vietnam all day every day. It was wonderful. But it didn't get rid of Vietnam. I found I needed to keep doing it, as I still do now.

Then with the advent of email in 1995, Vietnam invaded my life every day in my own home—and I wasn't at all sure I liked it. But I was stuck with it, and now, even though I'm on several Vietnam email groups, I think Vietnam is in an okay place. I read and write emails for an hour or so a day, and for me it's like non-threatening visits with friends and with myself as a vet. I don't have to completely divorce myself from being a civilian veteran, as I refer to myself, but I also don't have to drive my friends crazy by talking about it, or myself by stuffing it.

Coming home wasn't easy for any of us. Here are some experiences from other Donut Dollies.

Coming Home

In September 1967 I came back to the Real World.
From the train station I caught a cab to my parents' home
but along the way I must have been commenting a lot on

how different... how long... how cool... how...

Lady, where have you been!!

Vietnam, I chirped.

A quick look in his rear view mirror and he veered his cab toward the curb.
I pressed hard into the back of the seat where he couldn't reach
me to throw me out.

The cab stopped.
His hand flashed in one smooth slow motion—
palm up on the steering column shifting into park,
palm down in the meter's arm.

The meter stopped.
I pressed harder into the seat.
When he turned around I braced myself.

Welcome home, Lady …

This ride's on me.

J. Holley (McAleese) Watts

*Sharon (Vander Ven) Cummings described her home-coming feel-
ings:* I was physically and emotionally exhausted. I really didn't
know how to act. I would walk down a street and smile at everyone
because that was what was expected in Nam. Someone pointed out
to me that I shouldn't be smiling at everyone — it wasn't right and
people might get the wrong impression.

**I [Nancy] left my purse in the grocery cart while searching
the shelves because in Vietnam we'd walk into a mess hall to program, put our purse down wherever and not think about it again
until it was time to leave. Mother told me that that wasn't a safe
thing to do, even in our placid suburban town.**

Sharon goes on: I got very angry one day when I was in the
grocery store—there was this huge long aisle of cereal boxes. It

seemed like hundreds of different types of cereal. And it was more important to choose the correct brand of cereal than to think and worry about our guys who were being blown to bits on the news every night. Nobody seemed to get it that these guys were really dying and that was real blood. I got so very, very angry — and this was in 1967. I felt lost. I didn't know what to do next. Get another job? Nothing could compare to the excitement and fulfillment I had while working with MY guys in Vietnam. The letdown was very, very hard.

Another Donut Dollie had a similar story. She was walking through an airport (maybe on her way home from Vietnam) and saw two girls who were upset and pounding on a cigarette machine that wasn't working, ranting because they couldn't get their Marlboros. She wanted to yell at them, "Marlboros??? There are guys dying and you're worried about Marlboros???"

At a Donut Dollie reunion in 1993 in San Francisco I was asked to be on the panel about PTSD, in part I guess because I had been informed about PTSD by a Donut Dollie who had sent me multiple articles about it. I don't know what aspect of it others talked about, but I think I talked about symptoms.

As the panel went on, I noticed one particular woman in the first row who was very touched and emotional about what she was hearing. As soon as it was over, we went up to each other to talk. She hadn't heard of PTSD, but she was unknowingly living with the symptoms.

When the room was polled to ask if they would do it again, most said yes. When asked if they would want their daughters to do it, most said no. I've paid a big price for a wonderful, rewarding year, but I've gained a lot too. I've met hundreds of people my life would never have come close to without it; I've gotten a depth which I wouldn't have otherwise...but I've paid a price.

One of my strongest memories of the 1986 Chicago welcome home parade was as we walked along seeing a woman our age in tears on the sidelines. As I started toward her I noticed in my peripheral vision a veteran coming toward her from a different direction. I happened to get there first to give her a big hug, which I'm sure was his intention too.

As I left, I tried to tell the other spectators to take care of her because she seemed to be there alone. I hope they did....

I rode for a day with the RFTW many years ago, meeting up with them in Rainelle, West Virginia, and riding to DC. It was really really cool in many respects—riding with a large group of motorcycles, meeting such a variety of people, pretending to be a biker, and riding for a reason.

I have a key chain thingie that someone gave me that says Run For The Wall. No one who sees it knows what it means. Occasionally they ask. Sometimes I explain, and sometimes I just don't bother.

Here's a quote I've had on my bulletin board for, oh, 15-20 years.

"By then I knew that everything good and bad left emptiness when it stopped. But if it was bad, the emptiness filled up by itself. If it was good you could only fill it by finding something better."

Ernest Hemingway
A Moveable Feast

So how do you fill it if there isn't anything better?

It was in Danang about half-way through my tour, just after 8:00 a.m. and I was sitting outside the rec center in the Red Cross van with my best friend, just talking. The other girls had gone inside to get their days started—covering the rec center, going on runs around Danang or to forward areas, preparing programs. But Loretta and I just stayed in the van talking. We were there so long that Top, the middle-aged Vietnamese man who was our man-Friday for our various and sundry needs, came out of the center and unobtrusively placed two cups of coffee on the floor of the van. We talked about a lot of heavy stuff which I don't remember, but I clearly remember saying, "This will be the high point of my life."

And so it has been.

Families

28

Families bore the brunt of having a loved one in Vietnam. In re-reading these letters and tapes about my feelings about the war, the casualties, the mortar attacks, and my depressions, I wonder if I thought about the effect they would have on my family, especially my mother.

Ever since it appeared in *Life* magazine, I've had on my wall the David Douglas Duncan photograph of the tired face of a Marine wearing a steel pot with a short-timer's calendar drawn on it and a cigarette hanging out of his mouth.

And when his book *War Without Heroes* came out in 1970, I asked my parents for it as a gift. Mother's note with it said, "This seems a sad thing to send to wish you a happy birthday—particularly with the latest memoirs indicating the whole awful thing might have been ended in '67. But I know you want it, and I understand. These are the men who were there—they are all ours..."

I'm glad to have it, but it makes me too sad to look at it.

On the only MARS call I made to my parents there was a glitch in that we couldn't hear each other, so I asked the operator if he could pass on what was said. At first he said no because he wasn't allowed, but when it became obvious that we needed help badly, he did so. It was really awkward and hardly worth the trouble.

When my brother was killed, my family went into something of a shell, and although we certainly thought about him all the time, we didn't talk about him because it was just too painful. However, as far as our "positions" on the war went, although I made a deliberate effort to stay apolitical while in Vietnam, I was turning, or had turned, anti-war on my return. I attended a parade in San Francisco which I supported from the sidelines until the group chanting "Ho, Ho, Ho Chi Minh" came by at which point I left. I also considered joining VVAW.

My parents were fine upstanding patriotic citizens in an upper-middle class town. When they were being acknowledged at a Memorial Day ceremony, mother was crushed when protesters brought coffins. When Robert McNamara's book came out, mother was so upset by what he wrote that she couldn't talk about it. It seemed to be the summation of how her country had betrayed her. We all clearly knew by then that the war was wrong and lives had been wasted. (I use that word wasted with care because Billy's life was very important to many people and so was not a waste, but his future was lost and so wasted.)

All this is to say that there are many shades of experiences. There's very little black and white, and the shades of gray change depending on the person, the time period, the surroundings, the intent. How can I fault the Marine who was in Operation Buffalo and then joined VVAW in 1968? How can I criticize Doc for being so deeply hurt by protesters that he is caught in a struggle between his gentle nature and his outrage at deliberate mistreatment? How can I judge a protester as an unfeeling or uncaring person because he followed (and continues to follow) his conscience, as did so many others who chose a different course?

My parents have been interested in and receptive to following up on contacts with veterans and others whom I've met who knew Billy or were in the ambush. All those contacts have turned out very positively. My older brother, on the other hand, professes to be uninterested. He passes requests for information about Billy on to me or my parents. I pass information about Billy to my brother's wife, and I'm not sure how much she passes to him.

It makes me feel very alone in my missing my sibling, but I'm also very thankful for my sister-in-law's openness.

I've been to quite a few Wall ceremonies, mostly at the Memorial in Washington but also at Moving Walls, but this ceremony was special. Obviously it was special for us because it was personal, but primarily because the New Jersey Vietnam Memorial committee made such a commitment to the families—finding them, encouraging them to come, making them feel like it was for them, that they were the guests of honor. And I was particularly impressed with how the local veterans—the men who had grown up in New Jersey and knew the names on their memorial from childhood, who had been to Vietnam themselves—how they stood back and let the families come first. Veterans from a local VVA group were instrumental in helping with this, standing at designated points around the Memorial, ready to quietly assist the families in any way they could.

It may help to understand why this was so important to families when you realize that they, like the veterans, encountered the same indifference, disdain, and worse. My parents have been to several ceremonies at the Wall in DC (I kind of forced them to come), but they always felt out of place, like they don't belong—and people rarely recognize them for what they are—gold star parents. Grey hair doesn't trigger recognition like a uniform does.

During the months I spent in DC, I made telephone calls for the In Touch program of the Friends of the Vietnam Veterans Memorial, trying to find families of the men who had died so I could connect them with veterans who wanted to get in contact with them. The reactions I got from brothers were the most difficult. Some—many—just wanted nothing to do with it, and after a time I realized that there was just so much other stuff going on there—jealousy, guilt, anger, sadness, toughness, who knows. It got so that when I got a brother, I'd try to find a sister instead.

I've heard many times that the hardest time for the children of men who died was when they reached the age their father had died.

After volunteering at the Wall for several years, I noticed that the people I related to the least, the ones I couldn't seem to feel anything for, were the sisters. Once I realized that, I of course knew why. But....I couldn't do anything to change it. When I look at them, I think, I should know how they feel, I should be empathizing, but I usually feel nothing.

Joe Galloway was a correspondent in Vietnam where he was awarded a Bronze Star for rescuing a wounded soldier in the Ia Drang battle of the 1st Cav in November, 1965, when 305 Americans died. He and Lt. General Harold Moore wrote a book about those days titled "We Were Soldiers Once...And Young." These are the final paragraphs in the story he wrote about the battle and its aftermath in "U.S. News and World Report," October 28, 1990, "Fatal Victory."

The guns were silent at last. But 12,000 miles away, in Columbus, GA, the sleepy Southern town outside Fort Benning, the tragedy was just beginning to unfold. It was early in the war, and the Army had not yet formed the casualty-notification teams that later delivered and tried to soften the terrible news. The telegrams were simply handed over to taxi drivers to deliver. Some women collapsed at the sight of a cab pulling up outside; others huddled inside refusing to answer the knock.

Lt. Col. Hal Moore and his men had done their duty in the Ia Drang Valley. Now Julia Compton Moore—the daughter of an Army colonel, the wife of a future Army general and the mother of two sons who would follow their father to West Point—would do hers. Julie Moore knocked on too many doors in the flimsy thin-walled apartment complexes and trailer parks around Columbus—grieving with the women, comforting the children and wondering when the taxicab might come to her door. She never forgot one very young, Hispanic woman, pregnant with a baby who would come into this world fatherless. Julie Moore attended the funerals of all her husband's men who were buried at Fort Benning.

If you want to know the true cost of victory in the Ia Drang, ask Julie Moore.

I was in our backyard in New Jersey with my mother. It was not too long after Billy had been killed, and in my mind I was still in Vietnam. A helicopter flew over our nice suburban neighborhood and I looked up longingly. Mother saw the look and said, "If you have to go back, Nancy, go." I knew I never could—not only because of her but because the Vietnam I knew and the Nancy who had been there had died too. But it was one of the strongest expressions of unselfish love I've ever heard.

We Get Letters and Packages

29

Receiving letters was as important to the girls as it was to the men. Letters were also very important to families. I was so negligent in my letter-writing and later tapes, sending a total of about 22 over the 52 weeks, that a few times my mother gently chastised me. At one point, I was so bad that I received a "health and welfare" call from the ARC because I hadn't written home in six weeks due to a change of station from An Khe to Danang and just plain neglect. My parents had contacted the Red Cross, and I was told to write home. This was somewhat embarrassing, but at least I saw that the Red Cross notification system works.

Virtually all my letters home began with a version of: "Sorry I haven't written sooner. I've been busy, tired, hot, depressed, etc., etc." I usually didn't date my letters, so my family had to guess when I started and stopped writing each letter, often over a period of days. The dates given are often the date on the envelope. This is a long (and probably boring) recitation of my excuses and apologies.

Letter. May 2, An Khe

You're really lucky to be getting a letter because I am so d_____ hot I don't feel like doing anything except maybe read. I have the afternoon off after working in the center this morning and then again tonight. This probably won't be very coherent because I'm too hot to think—my brain has melted.

Of course, I forgot to mail this letter today so this is an addition at night. (The real reason I don't write more often is because I always forget to mail them.)

Letter. May 11, An Khe

I know it's been an age but I've gotten back into my old bad habits and I'm afraid they shall continue because on off-time I just don't feel like writing letters at all.

Letter. May 17, An Khe

I'm going to try to be good and write a little every night but if it bugs me too much (and I'm sure it will), I'll give it up.

Letter. May 29, An Khe

I've lost all motivation to write due to too much busy-work at the center.

Letter. June 27, An Khe

I decided to type this because I've been typing a lot of things for the busy-work here recently and I have become actually quite good (of course this probably won't last more than about two paragraphs). It's been so ridiculously long since I last wrote that I really don't know where to begin.

Letter. July 14, An Khe

Finally I have a free hour to write. The reason there is so little time is because whenever we finished work at about 8:30 or 9:00 I am always so hot to go party and relax that I can't sit down to write. Then I get in at 12:00 and am so tired and thinking about getting up at 6:30 tomorrow so I give it up. But I might try the business of writing a little every day.

Letter. Aug. 28, Danang

Well, I guess it's high time I wrote you [after a 3-week letter-writing hiatus].

It's now two days later and I am making slow progress with this letter.

Letter. Oct. 1, Danang

I just can't believe it's been so long since I last wrote you [this was after a 4-week silence]. In spite of the fact that I still really don't like it here, the time seems to go really fast because we have very little free time. We get up at 7:30 and work 'til 5:00 and then go out every night at 6:00 or 6:30 and then get back and plop into bed and that's that.

I started making tapes instead of writing letters and sent my first some time in November from Danang.

Tape. Dec., Cu Chi

I know I am a number 10 cow, which means translated from Japanese, I am a very bad girl for not having written or done a tape or anything for about a month and a half, but I think now it's just as well that I waited because after I left Danang and came down here, things were really miserable.

Tape. Dec. 22, Cu Chi

I'm really tired but I thought I better just record a little bit of this tape, mainly because I felt so guilty about not writing you before, you know, about that month and a half gap. In your letter it made me feel so guilty. I guess I don't realize how much getting mail from me means, even though I'm sitting here waiting for mail just the way you must. But time seems to go so fast here and I keep thinking, well, I'll write tomorrow, I'll write tomorrow, I'll tape tomorrow, and then tomorrow comes and goes and I haven't done it. It just keeps going on and on like that, but I'll try to be better now. I really will.

Tape. Feb., 28, Cu Chi

I haven't taped in so long because, well, things have been pretty busy because we have been short on girls, so there hasn't been that much to say, it doesn't seem like. Things are going pretty much as normal. [I then go on to talk about being mortared every third night or so – see Tet].

My sweet mother sent me numerous goodie boxes because I was constantly asking for things.

Letter. May 17, An Khe

In the process of driving out there [to the dispensary in town] I ruined a white blouse because of road grease which is thrown up and can't be gotten out. So if you have a chance, could you see if you could find me a white, cotton, sleeveless blouse, no collar, size 12. It was the only one I had and very handy—if possible one that can be tucked in or not. Just send it airmail in a big envelope—that would probably be easiest. I've lost (rather a girl I lent it to) lost my brown triangle scarf. Could you find another maybe—light tan because it's a good color.

Letter. May 29, An Khe

I got the blouse and it's perfect. I can't believe you did it. However, the scarf is not what I had in mind although it will do, but in the future what I want are the triangle cotton type—small babushkas, not the square chiffon or nylon type. But thanks a lot for both anyway.

Letter. June 27, An Khe

I got your package with the paper dress, earrings and scarves in it—all are great! I haven't been able to wear the dress yet because we had a huge rain spell and I decided it was just too risky! That was our first taste of the monsoon season and I think I'll be able to live through it.

The scarves are great and very useful because it seems like I wear a scarf about 90% of the time. If you should see any other cute ones (same style) in different colors, they'd be great. Which reminds me—I seem to have lost a whole pile of my hair ribbons. Could you check in my room and if they're not there, send me some more because I'm going to let my hair grow long enough to wear a ribbon. The colors I need are light pink, light orange, light blue in either satin or grosgrain, about yard long and this wide.

Letter. July 14, An Khe

I got your "package." It's so exciting to get them. The scarves are great altho I still need a light blue one and a pink one—the ribbons are fine—the earrings, the pink ones are beautiful, the cracker ones I don't know if I dare wear.

We're having a fashion show at the center which I'm doing when I'll show them and wear my tent dress. Which also reminds me—if you see any cute wild shifts, send them. The guys really love them and so do I!

More things I would like you to send me. (As I said to one of the girls today as I opened the package, "My dear mother keeps sending me little presents—she must really love me!) 1. another washcloth, 2. monsoon season is coming and the girls say the thing to have is one of those green army rubber raincoats, small I think but try it out, 3. could you send the perfume I have, Nina Ricci, Channel and numerous little purse-size ones on my dressing table and in my medicine cupboard.

I find I use a lot of perfume. We were with some guys on an LZ during mail call and one of the guys got a letter from his girl. When one of the others asked if it was perfumed, he said no, so I took it and dabbed some perfume I had in my purse on it.

Letter. Aug. 28, Danang

I have gotten various packages in the last few weeks which I can't remember if I've acknowledged or not. So here goes again.

The yellow dress is really good—I've worn it over and over again because it seems to fit many occasions. The brown one is really cute and so comfortable and I really like wearing it. The canned one is something else—that doesn't mean bad—it means like wild. I wore it the other night and got many disbelieving looks.

I'm kind of scared about wearing the wild dresses here whereas I wouldn't have been in An Khe because here we always go to a Navy officers club to eat and drink and some of the looks you get from the lecherous drunk men are a bit much. In An Khe I always seemed to be surrounded by friends and I felt at ease so that I could wear anything I wanted to.

Tape. Pre-Christmas #1, Cu Chi

The decorations are great. We've decorated our office with them and some in my room, and we gave some to some of the guys to decorate their area. So they're being put to good use. I also opened the package that had the mirror in it too, and that is really handy to have because I have this one pathetic mirror, so this is really nice. In fact, one of the girls came in to use my mirror the other night because it was so good.

Tape. Pre-Christmas #2, Cu Chi

You should see all the Christmas packages we're getting for the guys—the field director gets. I was looking at them the other day, and I got all goosebumps. The people at home are really nice to do this. Some of the presents are fairly expensive and some of them are really heavy and cost a lot to send, and some of them are from little kids. I got a really nice wallet from a little kid. It must have taken his month's allowance to buy it. And it really gives you a good feeling, this being over here and seeing the war shows you how much good there is in people.

I just thought of another present that I opened—kangaroo soup! I didn't believe it! I haven't gotten around to cooking it yet. It's going to be kind of hard to find a place to do it. Well, not too hard, but I am kind of scared about it. I imagine it will taste like turtle soup or something like that, but it should be an interesting experience. I'm afraid there are some other weird delicacies hidden away in those presents, but I won't open them yet. Oh yes, the steam pudding you sent. I saw it and I couldn't believe it. I was so excited and then I opened it and it had all mildewed. I was so mad, so upset. I kept the sauces so if you should perchance be inspired and can find a way to send it so it won't mildew, that would be great. I almost went ahead and made it anyway, but I couldn't do it. It looked awful, but it would have been so good.

Tape. Dec. 22, Cu Chi

I've continued to open Christmas presents, before Christmas, but I'm still saving some. One of the Christmas presents I opened was that radio which is really great. It really looks like a good radio, and it's nice and small. It will fit into a suitcase so it will really be practical and nice.

Tape. Feb. 1, Cu Chi

I got your Valentine's card, well, I got the package, the envelope, and then I got a Valentines card, but I haven't gotten anything in between, so I don't know if you sent anything or if it's gotten temporarily lost in the big mess, but do let me know if you sent anything important.

Oh, I need a couple of things which maybe you could send some time. Another lipstick—Revlon Soft Silver Pink, and deodorant, Mitchum's. It's in a thin green bottle and it has got to be Mitchum's and also some make-up. It's Cover Girl by Noxema, and the light color, okay? If you can't get what I asked, don't get anything because I want just that and just get one of each.

Last tape. April, Cu Chi

I loved all the Easter things. They are really fun. We had an open house here on Easter, and we used the bunny rabbit for the decorations and all the little eggs and bunnies, and then we took some over to the general's mess. We had some cookies left over from the open house and we took them over to the hospital and went in all the wards of the hospital. It was really great, passing out cookies and saying hi to the guys.

Mother sent goodies for the guys, too.

Tape. Nov., Danang

You've been asking about things people could send to the guys over here and the other day some of the girls came up with a really good idea which is to send sort of little packages with things that the guys would need, like soap and razor blades and even razors, and hard candy or something that would last or cookies if they could be packed right, and pens and paper and anything you could think of, and especially since it's Christmas, they could send something that had to do with Christmas. And the place to send it would be to the First Medical Hospital. The Marines really need it. So anything that you could send like that—little goodie bags in separate packages that the guys could use would be appreciated— even if you sent them to the Red Cross in goodie bags and then they could be passed out to the guys that needed them.

Get Over It

30

I have always resisted people who say, "It happened a long time ago. Get over it." Many of us who were affected by the war refuse to "get over it" because getting over it seems to mean forgetting. We/I see ourselves as "walking memorials" to those we loved.

The sister of a man who died wrote, "People have said to me that it is time to get over it. What they don't seem to understand is that my loss really has nothing to do with Vietnam but rather the loss of a sibling. Vietnam was only a small part of my brother's 22 years of life...he had a life."

Vietnam = the death of our brothers = our brothers. So this country's self-enforced and induced amnesia transfers onto our brothers. And for me, since I was also in Vietnam as a Donut Dollie before my brother went over, there's a double whammy with the "get over it" phrase.

But people who have lost loved ones in death in other ways, i.e., not Vietnam, are told to get over it too...move on, etc. Our society just doesn't deal with death very well.

I feel like those of us who choose to deal with death differently are beacons of light in a society in darkness. We may blink out for those who don't agree, but for those who feel similarly, or who are looking for some understanding, we can offer a light of understanding.

But having said that, I think about something I saw at the Wall which a vet had written. It said something like this, "Joe, I've carried you for 26 years. I will never forget you, but I can't carry you any longer. I'll come see you here and I'll remember, but I have to move on. I can't carry you any longer."

It's a fine distinction to make between carrying a burden and remembering. Maybe the difference is that someone else might view what we consider remembering as carrying a burden. And maybe for some of us the constant remembering can feel like a burden at times. I guess it's a call we each have to make for ourselves, and that call can change through the years.

Fort Knox

31

When I got back from Vietnam, I continued to work as a Red Cross recreation worker at the Fort Knox, Kentucky, hospital. I had gotten back in April '68, left the Red Cross and then reapplied about December '68. I think there was some question as to whether I could apply out of my region (NJ), but I expressed my desire to work in the south which I got.

I had a great supervisor—one of those older, single women who had been in the Red Cross forever and knew when to enforce rules and when to overlook them. I was the only DD who had been in Vietnam, but most of us broke some of the rules. We lived in the BOQ and weren't allowed to have enlisted men there, and certainly not patients. So of course we did. I'm sure she and others knew, but nothing was ever said. The only things I remember her saying directly to me about my behavior were that I should call the field grade women ma'am (which I never could remember to do not having been raised properly in the south) and not to wear my love beads where they could be seen while in uniform. The worst part was that I had to go by Miss Smoyer, not Nancy. Still can't believe I knuckled under to that.

She also had the good sense to give me the Vietnam wards. A couple of times she gave me a children's ward or the medical ward for the new recruits, but before long when she learned that I wasn't spending much time on them, without saying anything to me, both my wards were changed to the Vietnam wards and continued as such the rest of the time I was there. I don't remember her asking me directly where I spent my time in the hospital, but she had her spies out, I guess. She knew I was a good worker—I just had my priorities!

And then there was the time when I passed her coming to work, not wearing my hat as we'd recently been reminded to do, but instead faithfully carrying it. When I saw her, I slapped it onto my head—backwards—but I never heard a word about it. Cool woman.

One of the games I made up was "Name that Tune" for which I played the beginning of songs (on my pink 45 record player that I got when I was a teen-ager) and got the men on the wards to name that tune. I had that Kenny Rogers song ("Ruby, don't take your love to town") and always wondered whether I should play it. Sometimes I did, sometimes I didn't, but I always tensed up when I did.

One day I was playing the various records on the psych ward and as I played snippet after snippet, as happened sometimes on other wards the guys were getting a little irritated at not being able to hear the whole song. One loudly protested, "What are you trying to do to us." I hesitated a moment and then blurted, "Drive you crazy."

Fortunately they appreciated the sick humor. After all, they were Vietnam veterans....

The Wall

32

When I first started volunteering at the Wall, it was shortly after it had been dedicated in 1982 and had not yet become a tourist attraction. It was very quiet, unbusy, and the only people who came were veterans and family members. I would go to DC for a week or so once or twice a year, staying with a Donut Dollie friend who worked at the National Red Cross five blocks from the Wall. She'd bring me in with her in the morning, I'd spend the day at the Wall, and we'd drive home at night. I'd tell her what had happened that day and cry most of the way home. At one point she said, "I know this is very hard for you, but I know you have to do it."

My "missions" gradually got easier. I cried less, had some wonderful experiences, and got "better" at what I was doing. But I surely miss those days when emotions were raw, none of us knew how to act, but we connected on such a deep and immediate level. I keep trying to duplicate that.

In this letter to a Donut Dollie friend, I describe what my DC friend called my "combat assault" on the Park Service.

The Memorial was under renovation at the time. It was obvious that they needed help to assist the visitors since there was a fence around it keeping people away. So I went to the head of volunteers, a Park Ranger, who first said that it wouldn't be feasible for me to volunteer for just the 3 days that I was there—not cost effective, too much training needed, set a bad precedent, etc., etc. I was determined, so I just started talking about how I could do a good job of it, I'd been in Vietnam, my brother was on the Wall, and finally convinced him.

So I spent the next 3 days (in sun and rain) at the Wall. It was wonderful and terrible—a lot like Vietnam—very emotional and wrenching but at the same time rewarding. I wanted to do so much, especially for the vets, but I could do so little. But the few times they recognized my concern and thanked me for it, I almost cried. In fact, the whole time almost I was on the verge of tears—just seeing all that pain in the men and families. You could pick the vets out because they would come and just stare at a portion of the Wall for over 2 hours.

Anyway, after those 3 days, something finally clicked and I knew my ambivalence was over—I had to get back in contact with the men.

I *then go on to talk about getting involved at the Vet Center in various ways. And then:*

One other comment about the effects of my time at the Wall. You remember how the DDs who were there for the dedication [of the Wall] talked about that experience as being a closure? Well, I found that my 3 days there weren't a closure but rather an opening which is what I really wanted. I don't want to close it off in a nice neat closet—I want that most important part of my life, when I feel I was at my best, to be a part of me today, and that's what it has done—at least in a small measure. It's not that my PTSD is "cured" now, but I do feel like there is a light at the end of the tunnel (to use one of our favorite Vietnam clichés).

I met one of my favorite vets, a Marine, at the Wall because I was drawn to what he was wearing—a collared shirt, an OD field jacket with his three rows of medals.....and a tie. That was class.

I had an on-going "discussion" with a friend who worked at and around the Wall for years. The most he would wear to identify himself as a veteran was a small 101st pin. I told him repeatedly that he should wear his fatigues with his lieutenant's bars for these holiday gatherings at the Wall so that the guys would know that their officer who was with them then is with them still.

After a few years of total resistance, he was talking to another Donut Dollie at a Kokomo reunion who said exactly, almost word for word, the same thing I had told him. So he did, and has continued to do so, except that the last couple of times he's been wearing his captain's bars because he got promoted while in the hospital. So now I'm telling him to go back to wearing his LT bars because that's what he was—a platoon leader.

I love watching the care and concern I see vets showing other vets. The hand on the shoulder of a guy who's upset, the hugs when they find someone from their unit, the help finding a name or doing a rubbing—the feeling that I would die for my brother. I see so many there who need but are afraid of that gentle word that will tear down their defenses. Some let a little in and find it doesn't kill them; some are tired and are ready to let it go. And some just continue to tough it out, shrug it off.

One of the most touching moments I saw at the Wall was when a father came with his family. No wife but two sons and their wives. I helped him find the name and when I pointed to it, he fell to his knees. I had stepped a little off to the side and waited for one of the sons to be with him. When neither of them made a move, I put my hand on his shoulder. Then, finally, one of them did the same.

It's one of many times when I've seen that people just don't know how to respond at the Wall, and I certainly put myself in that category as well.

Another incident was when I was talking to a kid, maybe 12-13 years old, who was there with his school group. He was looking at his uncle's name and it was affecting him more than one might have expected. He got a little teary, so I put my arm around him. Then a vet who had been watching came over and talked to him. As the vet started to leave, the boy asked if he could hug him. Afterwards, the boy's friends who had been watching came over and awkwardly hugged him too. They just needed to see that it was okay to show emotions.

I was standing with a couple of chopper pilots in flight suits during one of the several days of the dedication of the men's statue at the Wall. Grunts kept coming up to them, thanking them for helping them out of bad situations. During a lull, I commented to the pilots about how meaningful it must be to get those acknowledgments.

They very quickly told me that they were grateful for the support of the infantry because they knew that if they went down, the grunts would be there to rescue them. A symbiotic relationship.

In the early days, they had performers at the Lincoln Memorial on Memorial Day. They were doing sound check/rehearsals the day before when I was volunteering at the Wall. I walked by and happened to hear Tony Bennett doing his sound check. He was just wonderful!

We riffraff were behind fences they set up at the bottom of the Lincoln steps, but he belted it out like we were an audience at Carnegie Hall. At the end, people were clapping, hollering, whistling. He waved to us, and we were as appreciative as if we actually were at Carnegie Hall.

Another great moment was when I heard wafting down to the Wall the strains of Michael Bolton singing in rehearsal. As a fellow volunteer said, "There's nothing like the sounds of Michael Bolton singing to us at the Wall."

And then there was another time when Billy Ray Cyrus was the star attraction. I went up to his entourage during rehearsal and asked who the singer was. They told me and I'm sure my face registered a total blank because I had no idea who he was. I'm from the 50s-60s, not the MTV generation!

One Veterans Day we Donut Dollies set up a Kool-Aid table near the Wall along with some photos of us in Vietnam. The local Red Cross chapter had given us Red Cross cups like we had in Vietnam and a container to serve the Kool-Aid. In Vietnam we often ended up serving mud-colored Kool-Aid because we had to mix several different flavors and colors because we never had enough of one. As the vets came by, we heard their memories of drinking it in Vietnam, and the best part was when one of the guys told us that what he remembered was the mud color.

A man was at the Wall with prosthetic legs and wearing shorts and veteran clothing. People were staring and taking pictures in a way I thought might be intrusive.

Since as volunteers we sometimes intercede for veterans, I went over to ask if it was bothering him. He said that no, people should see the cost of war. I then realized that he was wearing shorts so that people would see what had happened to him.

And then there was the time a lady about our age walked up to me when I was volunteering at the Wall and asked about the war, "Refresh my memory...what was the issue?"

Could have been a reasonable question under other circumstances. Under these circumstances, another woman standing nearby snorted and walked off. I was stunned and after thinking of several sharp responses, managed to just say, "It was very controversial and too much to go into here."

My encounter with Maya Lin [the woman who designed the Wall while an undergraduate at Yale] was memorable. It was when they were having congressional hearings about whether to allow a women's statue near the Wall. Maya was against it because, as I understood her position, there would be a proliferation of statues and the Wall was enough.

I was living in DC at the time and so went to the hearing. Several women were in the hallway outside, waiting for the room to be opened to testify, and there was Maya sitting down the hallway, by herself. I walked over to her to tell her how much I appreciated what she had done by giving us the Wall—and of course choked up while I was talking. She skimmed over that and said basically that she didn't mean to be against the women. She said more but since I can't remember exactly what she said, I don't want to paraphrase. But she was almost apologetic and very soft-spoken and modest.

I also saw her give a talk at the Friends of the VVM annual meeting. We, of course, wanted her to speak about the VVM, but she had moved on and instead talked about her latest endeavor.

Hard to know how the fear of peaking at age 21 feels. Or maybe not, since many Vietnam vets (and some Donut Dollies) feel that way.....

It happens during the busy veteran gatherings of Memorial Day or Veterans Day, day or night. It can happen at any time as people are looking for names, talking with others or just remembering. There's always a low buzz of noise, sometimes broken by laughter or an exclamation as veterans encounter friends. Movement is constant as people walk along the Wall, pose for pictures with friends, do name rubbings, tell stories.

But as soon as the notes of taps begin, played by a bugler standing in the trees or on the knoll, all movement and sound stop. People seem to go into themselves, silent and still as they remember. Sometimes kids or foreigners don't get what's going on, but they quickly realize this is a moment to pay respect. When it's finished, we take a deep breath, sometimes wipe the tears, and normal activity slowly starts up again as people try to shake off the effects of the moment and their memories.

One Veterans Day evening in the early years there was a wonderful POW/MIA ceremony on the knoll beside the Wall. Everyone was given candles—real candles—and after the ceremony people drifted over to the Wall with the burning candles. At that time period, we could walk anywhere—on the grass, above the Wall, wherever we wanted—so many people were on top of the Wall, including myself.

People began to place the candles at the base of the Wall and on top of it. After a little while, the word went around that we should not do that because of dripping wax or something. Policemen were around who I guess were expected to enforce it, but a slight rumble of noise started as people objected.

We wondered if the police would try to do anything, but as someone pointed out, half of them were Vietnam veterans. Nothing was done, candles continued to be placed, and the Wall was spick and span the next morning.

The only place I've seen photos of that evening is in the Smithsonian book, *Reflections on the Wall,* by Edward Clinton Ezell.

It was perhaps the most beautiful experience I've had at the Wall.

The Unknown Soldier

33

During past wars, a service member who died without his remains being identified has been buried at Arlington National Cemetery as an Unknown Soldier. Designation of a Vietnam Unknown proved difficult due to advances in DNA testing which enabled all the fallen to be identified. However, on Memorial Day, May 28, 1984, "our" unknown serviceman was buried. I had been encouraged to go by another DD, and it turned out to be a wonderful, meaningful experience which I describe in this letter to her.

Dear Jenny,

You were right—it was just wonderful—just as super as you said it would be. I'll start at the beginning. After Paula and I got to DC late Sunday afternoon, she offered to take me downtown because she too wanted to go to the Capitol rotunda. I was dying to get to the Wall as usual, so we arranged to meet Ann there afterwards. It was really nice in the rotunda—lots of all kinds of people, very solemn of course, and very respectful. Paula and I both came out teary-eyed and moved. We then met Ann at the Wall where we ran into two other DD's who had been there all afternoon. They too had had a super afternoon. They were wearing pins and parts of boonie gear, thereby making themselves identifiable, and about four women came up to them and said, you look like you were there, and started talking. Turned out that one of them was Linda Vandeventer [author of *Home Before Morning*] and they stayed with them most of the afternoon. Several of the guys were very supportive too. It was a difficult time for both of them since it was their first visit to the Wall, but they were really glad they'd done it and were feeling very good about it when we saw them which we were glad to hear since we'd been worried. That's what's so neat about the Wall; it really draws people together to be supportive.

As Ann and Paula and I were walking away from the Wall, there was a group of guys in fatigues who we had already passed when Ann spun around and went into her DD act. We wanted to find out whether there were going to be any vets walking in the parade so that was our excuse for accosting them (not that we really needed one). During the course of the conversation, one of the guys said he'd seen only one DD while he was in VN, so we pointed out that he was talking to three of them then—such a deal. We ran into some of those guys briefly the next day which was fun.

Then the next morning Ann and I and her 3 (count 'em, three) kids (one in a stroller with chicken pox) went back to the rotunda before the parade. We were able to stay inside for a long time since it wasn't crowded. We were both in uniform with Cav patches on our shoulder, and one of the guards walked by and under his breath said, "Cav men," and walked on. A little later he came back with another guard who had also been in VN and we talked for a while in undertones. The second guard had been in An Khe at the same time I was and he thought I looked familiar. He asked my name and said the DD he'd known was Nancy too—was there another one? Ann and I didn't think so. As we talked he remembered that the Nancy he knew had married a guy she met in VN so I knew it wasn't me. Later on in the day I realized that it must have been Nancy Warner and I've written her to tell her that she is still remembered!!

During the next couple of hours before the march started, Ann went with the kids to a friend's house nearby and I hung around waiting to meet four of the DD's and a Special Services woman. They all except two appeared in uniform which made us highly visible to say the least! We hung around some more talking to a few guys (not too many were in that area) and some reporter asked us what we had done in the war and we sputtered around and tried to make sense. Then the casket was brought out and suddenly we were on the run to keep up with it on its trek to Arlington. We immediately lost three of the girls, but the rest of us stayed more or less together as we walked beside the casket and for the rest of the day.

There was a large group (but not uncomfortably large so that we were crowded) who walked the whole way and we got to talking to some of them along the way. Margi hooked up with a guy who had been in Pleiku (as had she) who looked lonely. A nicely dressed guy (as opposed to the majority in fatigues or part of fatigues) talked to Ann briefly and then later to me after he had noticed me looking backward in the crowd to catch sight of Margi. I heard this voice saying, "she's back there with the guy in tiger fatigues" and realized he had seen me searching. We agreed that either the guy Margi was walking with was taking care of her or vice versa, but in either case, she was okay. I talked to him a little more later and quickly sized him up as good VVLP [Vietnam Veteran Leadership Program] material. He said he wanted to get involved somehow, so gave him Jeanne's address.

As we walked it was neat to observe all the people along the way (when we weren't frantically trying to keep up—Ann with her three kids, remember). It was a quiet crowd, naturally, and I didn't see too many tears, probably partly because we were right with the casket and the impact seemed to come slightly after it passed and there was time for reflection, but there were people all along the way. At the Wall the crowds increased and lots of people walked on to Arlington. As we got to the cemetery and were milling around after the cortège went inside, Ann (always the brave one) finally talked to two guys who we had picked out from early in the morning in the rotunda and who had also been walking the whole way. They were both really intense, said almost nothing to each other or anyone else, obviously were vets (one had fatigues), and were generally very interesting (and attractive!). Turns out they are Vet Center counselors from Maryland and we ended up sitting with them during the ceremony.

We all were ushered onto a big field next to the cemetery where they had a huge electronic television screen. Just as we were all settling in, a mass of vets in uniforms walked across the front of the field. They were the guys who we found out later had been marching behind because they weren't allowed in the parade. The crowd erupted in applause and cheers—really neat.

As we were clapping Margi tapped me on the shoulder and said there was a guy that wanted to talk to me. I turned around and here was this nicely dressed guy with red-rimmed eyes. When I shook his hand he started to say something about my 25th Division patch and teared up, so I put my arm on his shoulder and he said something about not crying. I said it was okay to cry and put my arm around him while he struggled for control. He said that he had been looking for a 25th Division patch and that he had never been to anything about VN before (or the Wall we found out later even though he lives outside Washington and drives by it several times a week and cries). I told him I was sitting with a couple of Vet Center counselors and would he like to join us—oh, yes. So he sat with us, and one of the other counselors and I talked to him through much of the ceremony to try to persuade him that his feelings weren't unusual, that the best thing he could do was talk about it in a safe situation, etc., etc. I think meeting and being there with him was probably the neatest things that happened the whole day. That's why I went.

After the ceremony (which I heard very little of) most of the others went to view the tomb while Steve (that guy) who had his van parked nearly took Ann and the kids and me back to her car at the Capitol. We all arranged to meet every hour on the hour at the flagpole by the Wall which we were all going back to. So then we went back to the Wall for a couple of hours and the rest of the neat part began.

My feeling, and it seemed to be that of lots of the people, was that now that the heavy painful part was over, the reunion could begin. It was like old home week with a bunch of people you'd never met before. There were lots of vets at the Wall (who probably had been there before so the initial emotional impact was over) who were there to visit and hang out, as were we. I went down there first by myself while Ann was with the kids and by the time I got to the apex I was surrounded by guys. We stayed there for a while chatting about times and places and units and whether they'd known DDs there, etc. It was really a kick—rapping the way we used to with them in VN and getting the same responses. I kept trying to remember that we were at a very solemn place and a lot of people might not understand and tried to tone it down, but it was hard to do. Other guys sort of joined in and there was a lot of outside interest as to what was going on in this group. I noticed a long boom mike trying to pick up what was going on. One of the guys said something about how it must have been hard for us to get a response from the guys in VN and I said it was a piece of cake— you guys were so great. They responded by saying they thought we were great too. Like you said, all those strokes which we need now which you knew we would get if we wore our uniforms—there they were.

When the counselors came back from the tomb, we talked some more. Ann met a nurse who had dated her husband in VN before he and Ann met—a really nice, warm woman who came up to me (a guy wanted us to meet) and gave me a big hug. When I told the counselors that Ann had met this nurse who knew her husband in VN, their faces fell. I couldn't figure out what was going on until I realized that they thought I meant that Ann and he were married when the nurse came on the scene. After reassurances, we got a chuckle out of it.

Another cute thing happened to Margi when she was standing in line for the drinking fountain near the Lincoln Memorial. A guy came up from behind her and planted a kiss on her check, and then said, "I've always wanted to do that." She told me the story later, and then as we were talking he walked toward us and she said that was the guy. So when he got up to us I said, "I want one of those too." He looked confused for a second and then said "Oh," and gave me a kiss on the cheek too!

Even though I got pretty tired near the end what with all that walking and standing, it was hard to tear myself away. The only thing that made it possible was knowing that I would be back in November—in uniform! It really was everything you said it would be. I think it made a big difference to all of us. I think the recognition from the guys and the thanks is what we need to heal some of our wounds and to bring about the closure or complete the circle or come out of the closet or however we each express it. I think it's different for us than the vets who need the acceptance from the country as a whole. We need it from the vets more than the country. I felt so proud to be in my uniform again and to identify myself with the guys again. I now understand what people mean when they say they feel 10 feet tall or say they were walking tall. I felt that way the whole time on the march. My posture improved and I felt great. It really was like coming out of the closet and feeling good about ourselves and what we did again. By wearing our uniforms, the guys know who you are. You don't have to talk to them and then take the risk of saying, I was there with the Red Cross or I was a Donut Dollie, and then wait for their reaction. Since they know who you are already, it's not likely that they would come up and say mean things, but only to be nice. However, we noticed that just like Vietnam, the guys were often too shy to come up and talk to us, especially if there were several of us. It was usually up to us to make the first move, unless there were several of them to give themselves courage. The little boy is still in them, which makes them so endearing to me!

A Day in the Life
of a Volunteer

34

*I had been volunteering at the Wall for about eight years when I
wrote this in about 1990.*

The volunteer is coming on duty. She walks quickly to the National Park Service kiosk to sign in, get the Directory of Names,
rubbing papers and pamphlets, puts on her yellow volunteer hat,
and starts toward the Wall.

Her pace slows as she pauses to acknowledge the statue of the
three fighting men with the thousand-yard stare and slows even
more as she leaves the hectic pace of the outside world to adapt to
the slower, quieter rhythm of the Wall. As she walks the length of
the Wall, she scans the visitors looking for anyone who needs assistance. She reads the letters and makes note of other items which
have been left by earlier visitors—a high school varsity letter, a
newspaper article, a Purple Heart, a picture of a squad of men in
Vietnam, many flowers, a POW/MIA bracelet. And so her day
begins.

A family comes down the walkway. The little girl is skipping
and laughing. Her mother stoops down to talk to her, telling her
that this is a serious place, the names of lots of men and women
who died in a war in Vietnam are on that wall and their families
and friends are coming to see their names. They continue on, the
mother holding her daughter's hand as she walks quietly by her
side.

A man with greying hair and wearing a business suit walks
slowly down the pathway. His body is tight, his hands by his side.
He looks only down or at the Wall, stopping occasionally. The

volunteer watches him go by, knowing he will be coming back. She hands out a few pamphlets, explains to a couple how the names on the Wall are arranged, and keeps an eye on the man. She looks up the name of a high school classmate for a woman, directs her to the name, offers rubbing paper, and watches the man. He walks slowly back and she goes over to him and quietly asks, "How are you doing?" He says, "OK," stops and quickly turns out toward the grass, fighting for composure. She waits and then says, "Is this your first time here?" He says "yes." And so a conversation begins.

They talk about the war and the people he knew there, the ones who made it back and those who didn't. She asks how he's been doing since he got back and he says pretty well but he has a friend—a buddy of his from Vietnam—who is hurting. She urges him to encourage his friend to go to a Vet Center and to bring him to the Wall so the healing process can begin. After talking for a half an hour or so, he prepares to leave, but before he goes he says, "I didn't think I wanted to talk to anyone, but I'm glad you stopped me." She gives him a hug before he leaves.

A group of three men are talking animatedly, exchanging stories, happy to be there together. After a while the volunteer goes over to them, curious about who they are and what brought them there. She learns that they demonstrated against the war and are now counselors of veterans. One does outreach service with Vietnam vets who live isolated lives in the woods of New England. As they continue talking, one of the men asks about her connection with the Wall and so she shows them the name of a Marine she knew and tells them the story of his death. The ex-protester rubs his fingers over the name again and again as tears flow down his face.

A woman walks back and forth along the Wall crying. The volunteer offers her a tissue and she stops to talk. She didn't know anyone who died in Vietnam and only a few who went, but the impact of the names has overwhelmed her.

Another veteran comes to the Wall for the first time after years of flying in and out of DC as a pilot. He was also a pilot in Vietnam. When asked why he came on that particular summer day, he answers, "Because it's hot and humid." There it is.

A group of veterans come. Most are wearing parts of their uniform from Vietnam. They are a Vet Center rap group and they have worked through to this goal of coming together to see their buddies on the Wall. They hug and cry and laugh and tell stories—and go away lighter.

A distinguished looking couple blend in with the other visitors. They go directly to a panel and a name and stop. The woman wonders again why no one from his platoon ever got in touch with them. She dabs her eyes, he puts his arm around her, they pause for a few moments and then walk off.

A 12-year-old boy stands crying among his classmates. The girls try to comfort him while the boys giggle self-consciously. The volunteer goes over, puts her arm around him and asks if he has a relative on the Wall. He shakes his head no, but says his mother's boyfriend's name is there. They go off together to do a name rubbing for his mother.

A young man walks up to the volunteer and shows her his silver POW/MIA bracelet. He says he's been wearing one for the past five years—not the same bracelet because he gives them away to people who show interest, but each bracelet had the same name—and he wants to find that name. The volunteer locates it in the Directory and takes him to it. She shows him the plus sign next to the name which indicates the man is missing. She tells him how that sign will be changed to a diamond if the man's remains are found or a circle will be drawn around the plus sign if he returns alive.

A group of women of varying ages slowly filters in. They are nurses and they inquire about the progress of the women's statue. They locate a woman's name on the last panel and one of the nurses tells the volunteer that the two of them were on the plane which was airlifting orphans out of Saigon when it crashed on take-off. Several of her friends are together on the Wall in the lines for those last few days of the war.

A man comes down with his tour group and asks for help finding a name. The man on the Wall was a neighbor of his family who used to shovel their walk. The volunteer offers to do a rubbing for him and as she finishes it, she asks if the soldier's family has been to the Wall. The man says "no" and so another rubbing is done for him to take home to them. And then a third rubbing to give to his own parents in memory of their neighbor.

Nancy doing a name rubbing at the Wall - photo by Daniel Arant

A jogger, face glistening, clothes wet, walks by greeting the volunteer with a smile. He pauses briefly at a name and goes on out to continue his run.

A vet in jungle fatigues bedecked with ribbons, medals, patches and pins stands alone in front of a panel with a single red rose. She can tell he's been there before and goes over to talk. He says a buddy of his was blown up over there by a grenade—it's the one death he couldn't get over after the war. But when he came to the Wall a couple of years ago, that settled it for him. He doesn't know why except that seeing his friend's name on the Wall with all the others made it final, resolved. But he won't forget, so he wears a black bracelet with his buddy's name engraved on it.

It's dark, her back is aching, she has a slight sunburn, and she knows her ankles will be swollen that night. She starts to leave, but sees a man coming along alone who might need help. Then his buddy catches up with him so she starts out again. A couple asks about the dates 1959 and 1975. She explains and gives them a pamphlet. There are only a few people there now. More will come later tonight when they can be alone. She takes off her hat, passes "her" name, and goes on out.

Pieces of the Wall

35

I wrote this in 1999 after I had been a volunteer at the Wall for 16 years. It's a compilation of incidences, all true, some of which are Wall Magic stories. Wall Magic is a term we volunteers have been using for years which came about because of all the amazing coincidences which occur at the Wall. I've had my own Wall Magic when three times while I was volunteering, people have come up to me to ask for my brother's name, not knowing who I was. We've heard these stories so often that when a visitor tells us, "I've just had the most amazing coincidence," we mentally shrug and say, "yeah, Wall Magic." They may have become relatively common to us, but we still love them!

A man stands by a panel where he has placed a large picture frame containing pieces of a boy's life—a picture of the young man in uniform, a newspaper article about him as a football star and one about his death, the letter from his Commanding Officer to the family. A couple comes up to look at it, and the man says to his wife, "I knew that man, I served with him." The other man hears him and tells him, "That's my brother."

A vet watches a young man staring at the Wall, touching a name. After a few minutes of hesitation, he goes over to him and finds that it was the boy's uncle whom he never knew. They talk and when the vet starts to leave, the young man asks if he could hug him. Afterwards, the boy's friends come back over to him and one of them awkwardly hugs him too.

Two men see another man doing a rubbing of the same person they are there to visit. When they talk, they find that the man doing the rubbing was his best friend in high school and the other two were his buddies in Vietnam. The vets say that they would like to get a message to his family, that there are people who still care. They tell the childhood friend that they have both named their first child after their buddy—both girls, both named Chris. The vets ask if the friend would like to know more about how Chris died and they go off together talking.

A young man with short hair and a fit body asks to do nine rubbings of one name on the last panel. It's his father who was in Special Forces and he too is a Green Beret and will be going to the Persian Gulf in a month.

A woman stands in front of her brother's panel. A man nearby asks a volunteer for six rubbing papers. The woman knows that when her brother was killed, 18 others in his platoon also died and so asks the man if he was a Marine and if he's looking at the same day. He says yes, he was in the same company, but doesn't know her brother or the man who died trying to save him. But he has buddies who are on the Wall with them and he was in the area at the time and so is able to tell her what happened on that day.

A vet is at the information booth trying to locate his buddy's name on the Directory computer. He knows the name should be there because he put him onto a chopper badly wounded, but it can't be found. While they are searching, another man comes up looking for his buddy's name which he too can't find. He had seen his platoon take devastating mortar fire at the LZ as he was being medevaced out. And then the two men realize that they are looking for each other.

A group of Soviet veterans who fought in Afghanistan come to visit their American comrades with whom they have so much in common in the wars they fought, both in foreign countries and at home. They place a folded flag from their country at the base of the Wall, and standing quietly around it, one by one place a red carnation across the flag. Someone speaks briefly in Russian and then they slowly disperse. At other times, Soviet Afghan veterans have left a cigarette, a shot glass and a piece of bread—the traditional salute to fallen comrades.

A vet sits in the grass on the edge of the sidewalk staring at a panel. A couple of times his friend, a fellow vet, goes over to speak briefly to him. Afterwards when they talk, he says he had gone back to Vietnam in his mind—so far back he didn't know his friend had spoken to him. Before their bus leaves a few hours later to take them back to Iowa, he sits down again with his buddies on the Wall—to say goodbye for now.

Moving Walls

36

There are several smaller versions of the original Wall in Washington, DC, referred to as Moving Walls. These walls are carried around the country to large and small cities and towns where they remain for several days. This allows those who can't come to Washington an opportunity to see the names and also to share memories with their hometown friends and family.

I've seen a lot of Moving Walls and it's been here in Fairbanks three times over the past 15 years. The first time it was here, when I walked up to it from the back as they were setting it up, I teared up. I'd been a volunteer at the Wall in DC for many years by then, but just being in its presence can still have that effect.

Working the computer at the Moving Walls is special because after a while you get to know the local boys, so when someone asks for a name, you don't have to look it up any more. You've got it memorized from having looked for it so many times.

One of the neatest things I heard was about a very small town in the mid-west. They had a different ceremony there every one of the five nights the Wall was in town, and everyone came. Many walked, and I guess some drove in from their farms, but everyone came every night.

At our most recent one here last year, John Devitt, the owner of The Moving Wall, said this was one of the few times he'd seen the veterans outnumber the civilians at the opening ceremony when they called all the veterans forward to stand in formation.

At another Moving Wall in the south (Dothan, Alabama) I was helping people find names on the Wall with a computer. They would come to the table, tell me the name, I'd look it up and tell them where it was on the Wall.

So a man comes up and says, "The name is (what sounds to me like Bail)." I asked, "How is that spelled," thinking Bayle, Bail, Bale, whatever. He gives me a look like, "How stupid can this girl be?" and repeats Bail (or whatever). I ask again, noticing in the process that his wife behind him is smiling and I wonder why. He then says, with that tone of voice that says, "Geez, she's dumber than dirt but I need to find that name," and spells B-E-L-L.

The light goes on, I feel stupid, find him the name and turn to help the next person, hoping I can decipher his accent.

I was working at the In Touch table at a Moving Wall in the south when a man came up to me with his "graduation" book from his Air Force fighter-pilot training class. He said he knew many of the men in his book had been MIA/POWS and wanted to know whether any had come home. As we sat in the back of the tent, he read off the names as I checked a list I had of returned (live) POW's. I get choked up thinking about it now, as I did then, when for many of the names I could say, "He came home."

The Wall That Moves

37

Talk I gave at the Moving Wall in Fairbanks, 2009

Amazing and wonderful things are going to happen at this Wall. People will come and talk about what they did during the war...what they remember about their lives or their families' lives at the time. They'll tell their family or friends about their high school friend who didn't make it back, how he was a special kid for whom everyone had great hopes, or maybe he was the kid who was always in trouble but everyone liked.

Those who weren't born yet—those for whom the Vietnam war is only history—will look with wonder as they see people interacting with each other—-and with the names on the Wall. Children will come with their fathers and see them cry for the first time in their lives. Wives will see their husbands tighten up, go silent—or maybe start talking for the first time in years about their war. Those same wives will think about all that they've experienced as they've shared the war with their husbands, often in silence.

Veterans will come at night, only at night, alone, for hours. Some will come and be unable to get any closer than the parking lot. Some will come with their families and wish they'd come alone. Others will come without families and wish they'd brought them. Some veterans will read about the Wall in the newspaper and struggle for five days—unable to come and unable to stay away. Some will read everything left at the Wall, others nothing. Female veterans will come, and no one will ever suspect that they served—that they too are Vietnam veterans.

This Moving Wall is a replica of the Wall in Washington, DC. For both veterans and civilians, it is also a representation of a wall that was built during the time of the war and during its long af-

185

termath here at home. For some of us, that wall went up in one searing moment—fully fortified and impenetrable. For others it was built one brick at a time, slowly getting higher and wider and stronger, until it too is almost impenetrable. Let's use this Wall to chip away at and take a few bricks off our old walls.

Veterans, take this opportunity to tell that person you've been working beside for five or six years that you're a Vietnam veteran. Give your family the opening to talk to you about what you did over there—how it felt then—and how it feels now.

Wives and children of these men and women, try to ask again and to listen again. When they show you a name, listen to the story. Listen hard. For you veteran families too—talk to someone about what it's been like for you as the wife or child of a Vietnam veteran. You'll find that you have more than you can imagine in common with other veteran families.

For those of you veterans for whom Vietnam was one year in your lives—a closed chapter that happened many years ago when you were a kid—reach out to your fellow veterans whose journey has been more difficult. Use this opportunity to look at your experience—what you gained and what you lost—and how that knowledge can assist other veterans and the community.

For those of you who lost family and friends, tell one or two people who didn't know about your loss and share your memories of your loved one. Families of men and women who came back, tell someone about how he or she changed—if they changed—and how you've dealt with it. And those of you who are here because you remember what it was like to be alive during the time of the war, or because you were too young to know but you've heard about it, tell a Vietnam veteran...thank you.

All of you—all of us—listen. Allow yourself to be open, to be non-judgmental, to hear the other person's story. Give your family, your friends, your acquaintances this opportunity to tell you something they may have been wanting to tell you for years. Use this Wall, this healing Wall, to take down, piece by piece, your 30-year Wall.

In a few minutes we're going to begin reading the names—every name. Each one will be read with reverence and respect. Each one is special—an individual. As I've talked with veterans over the years, I've seen the struggle, heard the anguish and the guilt as they fought to remember a name—but they just could not. Probably they never knew the name—we used nicknames, after all. Red, Shorty, Ski, Soup. The names are infinitely important—but the memories and the feelings you have about your buddies and your hometown friends are much more important. The names are there so people never forget those who died. You remember your friend—you've carried him in your mind and your heart for all these many years—but you just can't remember the name. It's okay if you can't remember. It's really okay.

And finally, many of us missed out on hearing something when we came back from the war. It's only two words, but there's a world of meaning for us behind them. So for those of you who didn't get to hear it or who didn't hear it enough, I would like to say to you, welcome home.

Return to Vietnam

38

In April 1993, I went back to Vietnam for a month with the Veterans Vietnam Restoration Project. Our group was small—three combat veterans and myself, a Red Cross Donut Dolly. We spent two weeks renovating a clinic at Cu Chi and two weeks traveling north to Hanoi. We worked and traveled with former Viet Cong and NVA soldiers which added an unexpected but very welcome and therapeutic element to the experience, especially since I was stationed at Cu Chi during Tet. It was an unsettling experience to be introduced to a fellow worker who was the head of the local veteran's group, learn that he had been at Cu Chi during the entire war, and realize that this man was lobbing mortars and rockets at me during Tet. However, during the two weeks we worked together on the clinic, we formed a special relationship in spite of our language difficulties. He gave me his gold star pin and I gave him a pin from the 10th anniversary of the Wall; we joked and teased and spoke of friendship and peace. His face became the face which humanized the enemy for me.

Vietnamese veterans we worked with at Cu Chi looking at pictures in
"The Tunnels of Cu Chi"

But, I'm getting ahead of myself. The most important thing that happened was a process I found myself going through during my first week there which caught me completely by surprise. My primary reason for going back was to get over the feelings of anger and animosity I've carried for the Vietnamese for 25 years. Although I was well aware intellectually that my feelings were for the most part irrational, I also knew that I wouldn't get over them until I went back. From my experience on other trips to Third World countries, I was pretty sure that those feelings would disappear almost immediately, which is, in fact, what happened. However, there were other aspects I hadn't foreseen.

Even as we were driving from Tan Son Nhut to Cu Chi, I found myself thinking "What are all these Vietnamese doing here; where did they come from?" and "Where are the GIs?" It was so strange and upsetting to see no American presence, nothing to indicate that we had ever been there. It made the whole thing—the war, the losses, the pain—seem even more of a waste. During the first few days I found myself getting more and more depressed as the guys in the group were getting more and more excited about how wonderful everything was. I wasn't interacting with the Vietnamese people on the worksite or getting involved the way I normally do when I travel, and I couldn't figure out why I was acting so differently.

Then, at the end of the third day, I had a revelation. I realized that I was mourning the loss of "my" Vietnam. As I thought about it, I was able to identify the stages of the grief. My denial has been in thinking about Vietnam as being unchanged since I left, complete with GIs and fire bases and choppers everywhere. Instead, I was hit in the face with a completely different country, a new reality, which I didn't want and couldn't accept. My bargaining has been that if I keep connected with vets and activities related to Vietnam, then the experience stays alive and not over. The anger I've felt has been toward the Vietnamese people, the Vietnamese government, and the American people and the American government. Those feelings of anger have spilled over in many parts of my life. And then there was the depression which I've dealt with in various forms for years, and which was hitting me full force again right then and there.

As I understood this, I knew that I had already dealt with the anger toward the Vietnamese people—that left immediately. And after working with the Vietnamese veterans and going into their homes and meeting their families, it was impossible to continue carrying my negative feelings. As I read *The Tunnels of Cu Chi* and crawled through the tunnels, saw pictures in every home we visited of family members who had died in the wars, visited the massive graveyards and memorials to the war dead, heard about the 300,000 Vietnamese who are still missing, I gained a compassion and understanding which I hadn't allowed myself to feel before. I had accomplished what I came back to Vietnam to do.

But even though I now understood much of what I was feeling and had even gotten over my negative feelings toward the people, I was still not at the point of acceptance. As I told the guys, I wasn't ready to give Vietnam back to the Vietnamese. But then after a week or so of being unable to talk about my changed feelings toward the Vietnamese people without choking up, I realized that it was over. I was done with Vietnam. Not done with the vets or with the aftereffects of the war, but done with the country and with the people. It's their country, they fought for it (on both sides), they earned it; and, although I now care for them whereas I didn't before, that part is finished. I still have all the other aspects of Vietnam (the war, not the country) to deal with, but at least one is taken care of.

Now I have two Vietnams—the one in my memory and in my pictures and in my vets, and the Vietnamese Vietnam. It had been "my" country for a while—my GI Vietnam—and yet it was theirs, and should have been, all along. I had been afraid of losing my Vietnam, of having to replace it with the "real" one, but now I realize I can keep them both—different but the same, separate but together, entwined.

So that was my experience. Traveling north after that was almost anticlimactic. It was wonderful to finally see Khe Sanh and other Marine fire bases, to get sand from China Beach, to go to the village near Danang where my brother was killed, to search for the Red Cross villa in Danang (which I never could find), to look for bullet holes in the Citadel, to visit the fascinating and disturbing war museum in Hanoi where the possessions of the POW/MIAs have been stored, and to just take care of unfinished business.

Other observations. The Vietnamese people really are as friendly toward Americans as I had heard. They carry no grudge that I could see. I asked several of the former enemy why that was, and their response was that they had been told by their government, and they firmly believed, that American GIs were not there because they wanted to be but because their government sent them, so that made all the difference in their attitude toward us.

After we had seen the museum and site of the My Lai massacre, our Vietnamese veteran guide told us that he didn't like going there because it wasn't representative of the American GIs, that this was an aberration. His son was killed at Khe Sanh in 1972 and has never been found. I will never forget the image of him standing on Khe Sanh with a Marine who had been there during the siege.

The Vietnamese veterans are very puzzled and curious about Americans' PTSD. When I asked whether they experienced it, they said no because they knew what they were fighting for, and their country's response toward them was totally different. However, we did observe some stress-related problems which is not surprising after 40 years of continuous war.

I recognized nothing. Oh, Marble Mountain looked the same, and I think I recognized a field just before a bridge in Danang; but I could have been dropped anywhere for all I knew. The NSA hospital is empty sand dunes, the bomb craters are mostly filled in (especially in the south), the rice paddies are green, cows graze on Khe Sanh (at least inside the perimeter—mines are outside), there are tons of water buffalo, the kids are a joy—and the war is over.

Nancy with children at clinic in Cu Chi

Post Script—I originally wrote this about a month after I got back, five months ago. Since the trip something has happened which I hesitate to identify because I can't believe it's true or real. I had listened skeptically as I heard others talk about a change in themselves after going back to Vietnam. And yet somehow that change has happened to me. Friends have noticed that there is something different about me—I'm a little more tolerant, a little less impatient, a little more open and less negative. Somehow the cloud has lifted a little bit—I feel lighter.

I've heard that when one feeling leaves, space is made for something else to move in. I know a lot of anger has left, but I can't identify what it is that has taken its place. I keep being afraid that the old me will return, and it may; but this reprieve has shown me there is another side, another way to be. That realization is what makes me want to share this experience with others in hopes that they too, might find, or make, the opportunity to let go of some of the pain.

My Return Revisited

39

There I was, sitting on the kitchen floor in Portland rolling spring rolls with some Vietnamese women (one of whom kept giving my efforts back to me saying they weren't good enough) for the wedding of a vet friend to a Vietnamese woman. Another vet friend told me later that he never could have imagined me doing that before my return trip to Vietnam.

I've had my 15 minutes of fame. Back in '93 when I went back to Vietnam, it happened that CBS with Dan Rather was in-country doing a program about General Norman Schwarzkopf's return to Vietnam. Somehow they learned that our group was there and decided they should have some other veterans on the program. So we sat on the roof of the Caravelle Hotel in Saigon at a long table and talked.

It was very hard for me to do because I was at a very emotional phase of the trip. I couldn't say the words "Vietnamese people" without tearing up, and I was determined not to cry on national television. At one point while I was talking, I choked. But at just that moment the tape ran out. The cinematographer did the fastest tape change in the west, and it gave me just enough time to regain my composure (and the General time to pat my hand and tell me it was okay).

But there were two things I wanted to say to the veterans, so I geared myself up beforehand, did some imaging of myself talking without crying, and did okay. One point I wanted to make was that women, too, were in Vietnam in various capacities. The second was about having been told to "get over it." I knew the guys were hearing the same thing and I knew the damage it can do. So I said, forcefully, "The war will never be over for me." General Schwarzkopf picked up on it and repeated that it wouldn't be over for him either. I thought later about how powerful that would be for veterans and their families to hear that this man, the Gulf War general, still carried his Vietnam scars too.

A few years ago (1993) our local paper wanted to do a short piece on me as a result of the Schwarzkopf/Rather TV program I was on briefly during my return trip to Vietnam. I originally declined, not wanting the publicity, but then decided it was an opportunity to "talk" to vets about the benefits of going back to Vietnam. So with great trepidation I said yes, but with several conditions. First was that it not be written by the 20-something reporter who first called, so the 40-something editor wrote it. Second was that a male vet be included (to take the pressure off me and add "credibility"). Next was that I get to read it before publication which, amazingly, he agreed to. It turned into a magazine-length article and took about two months to do the interviews and put together, an upsettingly long time of dredging up.

About a week before publication he showed me the article. It was very well done—very sensitively written, and he "got it"—except for a few things, such as he remembered the names on the Wall being in gold (interesting) and he called Marines soldiers (he thought it was kind of odd that I insisted on a change but he did so), and one biggie. He had left out the whole point for us—explaining PTSD and how to get help. We had the trump card in that we hadn't given him pictures yet which were a necessity for the piece. It was very tense—I didn't handle it well (one of those things where it was so important that I lost all tact), but the writer did and he changed it, albeit somewhat reluctantly.

All that is to say that I think details are critical—one mistake, especially if it's attributed to something you said, and you lose all credibility. Thank goodness the person who wrote my story had integrity.

When I went back to Vietnam in '93, our tour guides were former VC and NVA. At one point, after we'd gotten somewhat comfortable with each other, one of the Vietnamese asked me what the term that he'd heard meant—"gook." I was embarrassed and very hesitantly responded that it really had no meaning but that it was a bad word for the VC. He and the other Vietnamese veterans discussed it and then said with a smile that they too had a name for Americans—"yellow running dogs."

My impression was that neither one of us was the least bit offended. I guess in the case of foreign pejoratives, they have a stronger force for the user than the receiver. Seems like there should be a lesson in there somewhere......

The tunnels, the War Crime Museums and other museums, My Lai, etc., were to me very painful to visit, in part because of the truths told by them, and in part because of the untruths told by them. I sometimes got a sense of gloating from them, but other times (like at the museum in Cu Chi and at My Lai), I felt and heard very clear compassion from the female guides. I think it has to do with the differentiation that the Vietnamese people were able to make then and now, between the American people and the American government. As a result, they don't hold us personally responsible, even if we were there during the war. I find we Americans are a lot worse at doing that.....

For those of us who were there during the war, going back is not for the faint of heart. It's certainly not the playground which non-veterans might find it to be. But it's worth it.

Before we leave this round of the My Lai discussion, I need to tell my experience with going there in 1993. We were given a brief tour by a female guide who seemed hesitant about rubbing our noses in it. She said she would give us her spiel if we wanted but that, of course, it probably wasn't necessary because we already knew. I breathed a sigh of relief until one in our group asked that she tell us. I don't remember what she said, but I do remember the ditch—and the kids playing on the other side of it.

We were then taken into the museum, served tea and shown the guest book with a gentle suggestion that should we wish to donate, that would be welcome. I glanced at the book, didn't donate although another in our group did, and was just glad to get away from there.

I remember feeling very conflicted—appalled again at what Americans had done but not wanting to see it "exploited," although I understood at some level the Vietnamese need to address the horror. The translator asked if I was okay because of the way I was acting—just quiet and unresponsive. But it was all put into a perspective I could understand when one of the veterans in our group told me the comment of our VC/NVA guide who was traveling with us. He said he didn't like coming there because it wasn't representative of the Americans—that what happened there was an aberration.

I went into the tunnels and didn't particularly feel the claustrophobia—being bent over was worse—but still I knew I wouldn't have liked to live in them. The woman who showed us around the Cu Chi museum said that she'd been a young girl during the war and that they would all go into the tunnels in the late afternoon to spend the night.

When I asked about claustrophobia, one of the Vietnamese veterans (the one who was in charge of the Tet offensive in the area) with whom we worked on renovating the clinic said that he suffered from it and would chew beetle nut in order to be able to go into them. That was just one of numerous things we heard which made me realize that, as our group started saying as a sort of mantra, "we never had a chance."

The issue of people being missing was brought home to me, at least from the Vietnamese side, when I told a man at Cu Chi who had lost three brothers about my brother. His first question was, "Did they find him?" None of his brothers were found, as is true of thousands of their people.

This talk of massive graveyards brought to mind the one in the DMZ area of Vietnam. The first several times I heard its name pronounced, I thought they were saying Johnson. I finally realized it's something like Tron Son [Truong Son].

It's a huge graveyard with numerous markers, many without names. I was there with a former NVA who had fought in the area and also lost a son at Khe Sanh whose body was never found. He spent a long time walking the rows, reading the names. He found his unit but not, to my knowledge, any familiar names.

I tried to find our villa in Danang when I went back but couldn't figure it out, and of course, I didn't know the name of the street. The guide asked some people if they knew and someone said that some American women lived in the neighborhood, but still no joy. I don't think there would have been the lawn area outside anymore because all the houses were pretty much built up all around them.

Speaking of dogs, when I went back in '93, in Hanoi we were deciding where we were going to have dinner. Our guide took us down a dirt road lined with little shacks with a couple of tables and chairs outside of each one. Their offering was dog, or should

I say, puppy. Behind and beside the hooches were cages with dinner.

We took a vote in our group of four as to whether we would eat there. Two said yes, I was a no, and the fourth was undecided—until he thought about his dog that had been lost when he left the States and in sympathy, he too voted no. We didn't eat dog.

40

I struggled with what to "do" with Vietnam—how to integrate it into my life or put it away. In the letter to a DD friend after I had started volunteering at the Wall in January, 1983 and then at the Vet Center, I describe how it began to break loose.

I volunteered at the Vet Center for a few weeks before my job started and loved it. This has given me contacts with the vets around town which has fulfilled a lot of my needs. I'm feeling much better now that I finally did something. And I found that it hasn't taken over my life as I feared. It's a very large part mentally, but now that I'm working again, it can't be as big a part physically, but it's good to have an outlet for my feelings and thoughts about Vietnam. They don't bottle up inside so much and I know that the other guys who have their lives together also have PTSD, so it becomes just a given rather than a disabling ailment. Another thing I found at the Vet Center which made me feel good is that I can still make the same strong connection with the guys and they feel it. Of course, it's different than when we were all young and naïve in Vietnam, but it's still there. My concern for them can make a different in their lives, and that makes me feel good.

When I joined the email listserve VWAR in September 1994, I was able to engage with Vietnam and veterans on a different level. Although I had been in contact with veterans, those conversations were mostly about them and their lives. I was still stuffing my own feelings about the war and my brother. I wrote several pieces to the vets on VWAR trying to figure things out—my role then and now, my relationship with veterans, the way forward. Herewith:

Bearing Witness

I keep thinking about what I want from being on this email list. Do I want an audience, an outlet, a chat line, a laugh, a cry, to feel, to reexamine Vietnam (good and bad), to look at myself, at others.

There was a wonderful scene at the end of the movie *Witness*. The criminal was threatening to kill the Amish man when the boy rang the bell, calling the others in from the fields. They left their tools (potential weapons) in the field, came to the scene, and watched. They did nothing—they bore witness—and that in itself was enough to stop the crime.

I think that's what I want from friends, acquaintances— America in general. It's too late for them to take away the pain of Vietnam, or to prevent it from becoming full-blown in the first place. They had their chance and they blew it. So the best I can hope for or from them now is to bear witness—to listen when I want to talk, to be non-judgmental, to not even comment most of the time—but just to listen, to be there. It's too late for me—for them to do anything else. The "help" I want is, for the most part, from people who have been there, who have worn those shoes, walked those miles.

Now, it's easy to talk in absolutes. There are whole groups of people (individuals, actually) who fuzz the line. These are people for whom Vietnam and its aftermath have become almost as real as it is to the veteran--it's just a different reality. Not having walked in their shoes, I can't speak about their reality although I have no doubt that people who live with PTSD take on some of the symptoms. I'm thinking mainly of women who live with veterans, but there are others, like friends, families and counselors. But still, I wonder (and I don't know about this, but I wonder) if the best they can do for their veteran is to simply bear witness. Some of the best listening I've had has come from these veterans of another kind of war.

I don't mean to imply that the veteran is the only one to whom this care and attention is due. As we've said many times on this list, pain is pain. One person's pain doesn't diminish another's. And I guess the best we can do is to try to be strong enough to hear that person's pain—or less dramatically, hear their story. Bear witness. And maybe, just maybe, by bearing witness some of the pain will go away.

After writing this a few days ago, I read an article by Jeffrey Jay, Director of the Center for Post-Traumatic Stress Studies & Treatment in Washington, D.C., called "Walls for Wailing" ("Common Boundary," May/June, 1994). He addresses the response of the Jewish people to hundreds of years of trauma. His premise is that because the Jewish religion has traditional ceremonies, both at the time of the trauma or loss (the Kadesh) and at regular intervals throughout the year which are participated in by the entire Jewish community—because of this sharing and recognition, the victims are not isolated in their grief and so are better able to integrate it into their lives.

The contrast between that and the experience of Vietnam veterans is obvious. It occurs to me, though, that veterans have instead formed their own community, comprised of themselves and others who choose to share the trauma, complete with their own Wailing Wall and ceremonies like those on Veterans Day.

I've been thinking about what Ghost said about revisionists, wondering if that applied to me. I'm not quite sure what the term means, but I think it has to do with changing history, or maybe just the way you look at it.

I know I certainly don't want to change the facts of my Vietnam experience, although I may want to change the way I look at it. I don't want to change the way I remember myself as I was then, and even more than that, I want to hold onto the way I remember the guys. I don't want to revise my happy memories, making them sadder or happier than they were. And I don't think I want to erase the sad memories, although they have faded with time.

But I know I do want to revise the way I think about Vietnam now—as an adult. I revised it in a big way when I went back to Vietnam, leaving the feelings of anger and worse that I had felt for the Vietnamese, and instead allowing myself a different way to think about them—a way which made me stronger instead of weaker. I still slip back—I see an Asian face or hear Vietnamese and there's a jolt of the old feelings, but I have a rational response I can use now—a way to say, "That's changed. Remember?"

Vietnam has held me in its grip for over 20 years and I finally realized several years ago that I don't want to "get over" that. That grip has tightened considerably since I've been on this email listserve, but it's different now. It's not so much out of my control the way it used to be since the grip is shared by others. It holds us together instead of me apart. Sometimes it's a gentle pressure and sometimes it squeezes til it hurts. It squeezes words and thoughts out of me which I didn't know were there or hadn't bothered to formulate. It helps me to revise and change, to grow with this presence which seems to have been with me all my life, and which I know will never leave.

ReallyCares is an expression coined by one of the VWAR participants to describe people who express, to the point of gushing, excessive sympathy for veterans.

I've been thinking about this issue of being a ReallyCares as it relates to me and Vietnam. The reason I went to Vietnam is because I reallycared, and it seems to have been imprinted in my soul. I have tried to transfer those feelings to other parts of my life; I've tried to stop reallycaring, thinking that then I could move on, whatever that means. But it doesn't seem to go away.

I finally accepted seven or so years ago that Vietnam was never going to go away, and that was okay. But I still didn't know where to put it or how to control it. So I decided to go to Washington and spend several months "doing Vietnam." Being there was great but it didn't work—I'm still going and still doing it.

When I work at the Wall or do In Touch it's in my reallycaring mode. I don't do my stuff, whatever that is. So I've tried Vet Center groups, but it's so hard to be a woman, especially a Donut Dollie, in a group of men, most of whom are combat vets. Nothing that happened to me in Vietnam is as bad as what happened to them. Yes, DDs have their own form of survivor's guilt, so I keep trying to do more because I couldn't do enough then and what I did then doesn't really count, and there's sure no way to do enough now—the pain is too deep and too long-term.

I think part of the reason why I decided to get onto this email list, even though it's invaded my refuge much more than I could have imagined, is that I hoped it might be a place where I could have contact with vets out of my usual role. I can hear your stories, and maybe I can tell mine (although I really don't have any to tell) without seeing or thinking I'm seeing eyes glaze over, or feeling like this is so insignificant in comparison. It would be nice to find a spot among vets and not be a ReallyCares but just someone else who was there and who hasn't forgotten. I don't see this place as the answer, but maybe a partial means to an end.

I've thought about the "dangers" of telling personal stuff on here to hundreds of people. My first reaction, as usual, is, "What are they going to do, send me to Vietnam?" which has a way of putting things into perspective. And I guess I figure that I would say any of this in person to any of you if I thought you were interested (but you'd have to convince me first). If I get comments that hurt my fragile little ego, then I can put it in perspective that there are those who know what I'm saying. If you're not interested, I won't know. If I get silence—well, I guess that's the worse. (Do I sound like I'm trying to talk myself into sending this?) Do I want back ReallyCares comments? Yes and no. Yes, it's better than nothing, but no, I'd rather be heard than comforted.

I just have to say that using words like "warriors" and especially "heroes" makes me cringe—and makes me very angry. It shows a lack of understanding about those men (and women)

who were over there, why they went and how they died. And it has the potential of adding to the guilt and feelings of inadequacy to other veterans, including those who serve today, because they/we know that we weren't always warriors or heroes.

As an example of what I base that on—a vet friend of mine declined to do the voice-over for a Vietnam video in part because of the use of the word "hero" in the narrative. And from my personal experience, I would never refer to my brother as a warrior or a hero, although he was a Marine who died fighting for and with his men.

It's important to point out, though, that among Native Americans the term "warrior" is used very differently than others use it. That may be true for other cultures as well. I have no doubt that if veterans had been brought back the way Native Americans were to their families and nations (using whatever terminology was appropriate to that culture), we'd have all been much better off.

Correct me if I'm wrong, guys, but throwing your medals back at the White House didn't necessarily mean you (they) weren't proud of your service. It meant they didn't like the policy, it meant they didn't like seeing their buddies left in the field, it meant they no longer wanted to be associated with a government that gave them medals that cost them and their buddies' lives and limbs for no reason. It certainly doesn't mean they weren't proud to have served with the men they did, just as I was proud to be associated with the Marines and the 1st Cav and 25th Inf. Div. and all the others.

And if, in fact, they are no longer proud of their service, it's not because of what they did—it's because of the way they were treated when they came back. The bitterness that suffuses everything isn't related to their buddies, unless it's the travesty of having them blown away, either before or after the war.

There was no way, then or now, that I could say to a veteran that all the losses he suffered were pointless or for nothing or a waste. Nor could I say the opposite. As one vet said when he heard someone say, "What a waste," while looking at the names on the Wall, his buddy's life was not a waste.

Thanks

41

We didn't expect or even want to be thanked in Vietnam. After all, we were all in it together. I remember only a couple of times when someone did and it was very special, but it makes me feel awkward when guys say it now. We did what we did because we had to...for ourselves. And I think that sometimes the difference we made wasn't even that we did anything, but that we were a witness to what they did. Just standing and watching, being there with them, is a validation in itself.

Several years ago in DC during one of the Veterans Day weekends, a man came up to me when I was wearing my Red Cross uniform. He'd been a medic and he told me about an incident which has haunted him. Although I can't remember the details, it had something to do with a bad day (and a bad day for a medic is very bad), Donut Dollies being there handing out ditty bags, and a rude, gross comment he'd made to her.

It had bothered him all these years and he wanted to apologize to a DD. He gave me his combat medic's pin by way of apology and the next year when I saw him I gave him a Red Cross pin.

I figure those guys have carried so much that I hate to think that things they said to us under stress have added to their burdens. On the other hand, if I'd been on the receiving end of one of those really harsh comments (I only got a few mild ones), I wonder if I'd still be carrying it.

WHO KNEW...

That so many would smile and welcome us because they said
...we reminded them of home.

Some got angry and told us to leave, that we didn't belong there,
...we should have stayed home.

Eventually, I realized it wasn't about us at all but who they'd become
...since they left home.

J. Holley McAleese Watts

About glazed eyes and the thousand yard stare—yes, I know that stare, but I think it's more than that when guys talk to us. I think they just really have a hard time relating to what we did over there and why. Heck, I have a hard time believing it myself. I mean, a girl on a firebase in a blue dress playing games! Now I ask you!

I met Ken Willis and his wife while volunteering at the Wall during the dedication of the men's statue in 1984. I don't remember our conversation, but we must have talked enough that I gave him my email address. I later received the following message from him.

Dear Nancy,

So nice to meet you. I just wanted to drop a line to share a few old memories with you.

I was in the 1st Cav from May to May, '67 to '68. I visited the Red Cross Center at An Khe in May of '67. I was new in country and going through the in-country training program at An Khe. Our sergeant took us over to the Red Cross Center one day just after we finished the ten-day training program. We were on our way out to the field the next day.

Anyway, there is this memory about Red Cross Donut Dollies you might enjoy. It occurred on Christmas Day of 1967. My unit, 2nd of the 8th, was at L.Z. English in the Bong Son. My squad was detailed to some escort duty that morning and when we returned, we ended up being the last people through the chow line.

I was the last guy to be served and there were these two Donut Dollies helping serve Christmas Dinner. Well, it was really pleasant to see them and I shared a few pleasant words with both of them. Then as soon as I got my chow I went to sit down with some of my men in an area not far from the mess tent.

To my wonder and amazement, the two Donut Dollies came over and sat next to me with their Christmas dinner. All of us were so pleased that these two young ladies chose to be with us instead of going to the Officers Mess, we couldn't believe our luck!

After we finished eating, I asked the gals if they wanted to have a tour of the L.Z. (L.Z. English was pretty big, it was the forward command for the 1st Brigade.) Anyway, they said yes. So another fella and I went out and "acquired" a jeep so that we could give them a ride. (What the hell, the Brigade Sergeant Major wasn't using it anyway).

We had a wonderful time together. It lasted an hour and a half to two hours. Here were these two Red Cross gals in a jeep with five or six G.I.s, (remember, those jeeps were only supposed to seat four) getting a tour of the L.Z.

Both of them were very sweet to us. They smiled and joked and acted like everything we said was important. To my utter amazement, my squad mates actually cleaned up their language! It was all great fun.

Then it was time to take them back to the air strip for their flight return to An Khe. We all stayed with them right up to when they got on the plane (a C-130) and waved good-bye. For a long time I tried to remember their names.

I saw one of them again a few months later. She had given me her name and told me to stop and say hello the next time I was in An Khe. I looked her up.

We had dinner in the officers' mess at the hospital. (I was a Buck Sergeant E-5, but this gal told an Army doctor that I was a LT so she could get me in—I wasn't wearing my stripes at the time). We saw a movie over at the hospital and had a beer together.

It was an innocent visit, and she was as sincere and as kind as before. I can't remember her name today, but I will always remember that special Christmas Day, and how wonderful those two young women made me and my buddies feel by just simply being there and being nice to us.

The experience with the ladies was more poignant when I recall that only a few days before that Christmas, we had just ended what was later called the Battle of Tom Quan. It was a nasty drawn-out fight that went on for about ten days in the Bong Son. One day you're in a fox hole dodging bullets and a few days later you're sitting on a rock talking to a girl from back home. It was an amazing war.

As I look back on that occasion, I often wonder if those gals knew how all of us treasured each one of their smiles? I bet they knew. Considering the place and the time. The simple fact of their being there to smile and laugh with us was the greatest Christmas gift we could have ever wished for. Not all of the young guys who were in our lucky group that day came home. One of my fellas was killed in the Tet Offensive just one month later and another in the A Shau Valley a little later on. I'm glad they had a few hours to laugh and tell a few jokes with a couple of great gals on Christmas Day.

Anyway, thank you for going to Nam in the Red Cross. You and a lot other young women like yourself gave small treasures of relief to fellas who wondered if they would ever live to see another Round Eye, let alone talk to one. I know it was hard on you, it was hard on us all. But you were special, because you really did not have to be there at all.

Thank you,
Ken Willis, Upland, CA
2nd Bn, 8th Cav, 1st Air Cav., 5/67 to 5/68

My response:

It's nice to hear from you, Ken, and thanks for the nice words about the Donut Dollies. You know how it is, even after all these years, we still need to be told we made a difference; kind of like you guys never got your welcome home, we like to hear that you remember us. Does that make sense? It does to me anyway!

I'm so glad to hear that you had such good, and what I like to think of as typical, experiences with the DDs. All the stories we hear about eating only with the officers, dating only officers, etc., etc. just weren't my experience. I sat with the men for meals at LZs whenever I could (sometimes we too were pressured so much we couldn't); I tried to talk to everyone although there were times when I was so hot and tired that I just really didn't want to see another GI; I got up at 2:00 am to serve breakfast to guys going out; I loved being around the men—it was a privilege I've never gotten over. Which is why I still like to hang out with them/you.

[An officer told me after the war that the officers were told not to come to our programs or interact with us because it was time for the men.]

And I asked if I could share his letter with the Donut Dollie email group. His response:

As far as sharing the story, of course. It has a meaning and I was sincere about what I said regarding the Red Cross Girls. There are more than a few ladies who should know that their being there was important to a lot of young fella's who needed to see them and speak to them. I think seeing you gals had a civilizing impact on us.

I can also tell you another story, though less dramatic.

One day I was taken out of the field to go on R&R. I arrived at the air strip on L.Z. English to go to An Khe. It was a hot day. I hadn't been able to bathe in a week. There was a tent set up for people waiting to get on the C-130's or Caribou's (or whatever else was flying). When I walked up to the tent I discovered two Red Cross Donut Dollies sitting down in the shade waiting for what would be the same plane. I was carrying full field gear with 500 rounds of M-16 ammo, my rifle (of course) and a bunch of fragmentation grenades. As I began putting the grenades into a box located for that purpose (a sign read "deposit all grenades before getting onto flight"), one of the gals spoke to me and asked if I would like to play a hand of cards with her and her buddy. I said sure!

A few hundred yards away a C-130 was being loaded with silver containers. One of the girls asked me, "What is that over there?"

I looked up and knew right away. "Those are coffins containing KIA's."

The gal looked embarrassed and sad, both at the same time. We didn't discuss it any further.

The card game, somewhat somber now, lasted for half an hour or so, and then our plane pulled up.

We got on the plane and flew to An Khe. When we landed in An Khe, a sergeant from my battalion was waiting with a jeep. We gave the two gals a ride to the Red Cross Center and said good-bye. Then the other sergeant and I were off to the 2nd of the 8th.

Point is, despite the fact that I smelled worse than something the dog drug in, looked like hell warmed over and was too embarrassed by these facts to open a conversation with these gals, they spoke to me. They made me feel like a human being and shared their regard with me. The circumstances did not matter. They knew what the score was (that a lot of young guys like me were hanging by a thread) and they were there to pass out a little civility and good cheer. It meant something. I appreciated it. Still do.

And then there's my exchange of emails with V-man shortly after I joined the veteran email group, VWAR, my "coming out."

19 Oct. 1994

Hey Nancy..............

I've wanted to say something to you ever since you came in. I'm not really shy. Ask anyone. I don't know what it is. I've never talked to a Donut Dollie. Oh I've seen you, all right. I could not believe it when I did, but you were there. You saw me too. At Firebase Gladys - on the Song Dong Nai. That firebase was the most forlorn in the 199th LIB while I was there. Access only by air. Charlie's country in the Iron Triangle on the border of War Zones D & C. Round-eyed wimmen! Who'd a thunk it? You people were insane. I still cannot believe that you went there.

When we worked out of Gladys, Death walked with the squad every time. It was a bad place. And the Donut Dollies came there! They were VOLUNTEERS. Nancy, I can't give you a higher compliment. The Country that can produce young women who will volunteer to go to places like Gladys to try to help has my allegiance. The women have my allegiance. You have my respect.

They told us you were coming. We didn't believe it. The wreckage of one of the last choppers lay within a stone's throw of the firebase. The whole place was only as large as a football field - if that large. We swam in the river only if we set up a manned 60 for snipers. There was so much Agent Orange runoff from WZ D on the other side that we got sores on our bodies after we swam - we didn't know any better. It made the snipers a lot easier to spot over there. Maybe. That's why we used it on our perimeter too. You landed in it on the makeshift pad outside the wire. Sorry 'bout that. They said you would come - but we couldn't believe.

I felt the whump, whump, whump of your chopper in my chest before I heard it. It was always like that for me. Still is. I don't remember if this was before or after my close encounter with the mortar shell that destroyed my hearing among other things. Then we saw it. Huey. It looked full. Not full like us comin' back in but full for non-combat purposes. You and two other Dollies got off along with a couple guys with 16's and some civilian lookin' guy in new-green fatigues. Then came the pilot and the oscar and a gunner or two. It's hard to remember 'cause all we really saw was the Donut Dollies.

As we let you thru the perimeter, our eyes met for an instant. You likely don't remember since all the guys were lookin' at you Dollies an' nuthin' else. Charlie coulda taken us then. Except we woulda torn him a new asshole protectin' you. That's as close as we ever got, you & I. I'm one of them who sorta drifted away and watched. I had been there too long by the time you arrived, I'm afraid. No trust left in me. I wanted to come up and say Hi and gaze into your round eyes. I knew I couldn't trust myself around real people anymore.

You say you don't think you did enough over there, huh? Bullshit! You were the only thing/person I encountered over there other than my brothers that gave me any reason to care anymore. I figured that if you would come, of your own volition, to that place where death was just one crack of a rifle away, then there was still goodness afoot in the world. You were as alien to us as we probably were to you but you put, way down deep in our hearts, a small spark of hope. I know it didn't always show. I know it hardly ever showed - but you helped us.

Nancy, the glazed look you see when you tell your stories is the thousand mile stare. They aren't tuning u out because you are of little consequence. Your story reminds them of something - like any other of their brother vets stories would and they zone out a bit into their particular world.

We do that. I do that. You do that too, huh? Maybe you got more in common with us vets than you have been giving yourself credit for. Son-of-a-bitch woman - you Donut Dollies came to Firebase Gladys to try to cheer us up!!

To my way of thinking, you all did much more than was expected. I know that this doesn't make the survivors guilt go away since I am wracked with it myself. Just know that you did all you could in an important role.

Nancy, you know I'm speaking generally when I use the term 'you' about being at Firebase Gladys (unless we were there at the same time). I don't know who the Donut Dollies were who were there but I've always wanted to thank them. Thank you, Nancy, for doing the things for us that you did.

You must have seen guys like me who leaned back against the side of the berm and watched from afar. Did you think they didn't care? Did you think they thought YOU didn't belong?

That's what I thought they were thinking about me until I became one myself. I/we were wresting with our own demons in our own little worlds.

We looked at you and knew. We were the ones who didn't belong - back in the world where you came from.

Welcome Home, Nancy
Peace Sister,
V-man

ps - what r they gonna do? send us to nam?

And my response:

Yeah, V-man, I saw you. I saw you at every firebase I flew in to, I saw you when I visited in the hospitals, I saw you when I served meals at the mess halls or chow lines, I saw you when we took Kool-Aid to the flight lines, I saw you when I waved back at you after getting off the chopper, I saw you at the stand downs, in the bunkers, along the road, in the recreation center—I saw you everywhere.

I hoped that you were just staring because you were too shy to talk or too stunned at seeing round-eyes. I hoped it wasn't because (as a dear friend told me later when I got to know him while he was recuperating in the Fort Knox hospital where I worked after I came back)—I hoped it wasn't because you didn't want the "tease" of talking to an American woman you couldn't get close to (but if it was, I understood that). I hoped it wasn't because of those rumors, those soul-destroying rumors that sent so many women into the closet.

I knew it was because you just didn't know what to say. You were like that cute little guy I talked to at a stand down, drunker than a skunk but thrilled to be talking to a round-eye, whose every other word was a swear word and every third word an apology. Or are you the guy I saw again in the hospital after his second wound who kept saying, "I don't want to go back out to the field, I don't want to go back out to the field." Maybe you're the Marine in intensive care who I walked out on because I just couldn't take it (DDs had the luxury of leaving, nurses didn't). Or are you the one who came by the table in the PX where another DD and I were having a coke, feeling rotten for having just left ICU, who said, "I just want to thank you girls for being here." Are you the vet I saw at the Wall on that veterans' weekend who bounced up, kissed me on the cheek and said, "I always wanted to kiss a Donut Dollie." Or one of the ones who just say, "Thank you," which brings tears to my eyes, as I struggle to accept the thanks and simply answer, "You're welcome."

No, that's right, you're the one that just stood by the berm and watched, with the beginnings of the thousand yard stare, the one I couldn't get to, the one whose pain was already too deep, the one who won't let me go.

Yeah, I remember you.

The Saga of Crinkly Eyes

42

It was a Veterans Day weekend, the 1993 one for the dedication of the Women's Statue. I was walking into a hotel where many veterans were staying when I heard a voice say, "There she is." It was a veteran I'd met several years earlier, pointing me out to one of his men, a Marine, an amputee. The guy asked me if I was Lucy Caldwell, a question that left me stunned.

I knew Lucy, not because of Vietnam but because she came from my hometown, Princeton, NJ, and my parents had known her and her husband for years. Charlie Caldwell had been a football star and later a coach at Princeton University before he died. When the war began, Lucy, a middle-aged woman, had spent four years in Vietnam as a USO worker in Danang. During my tour I had run into her several times, and Marines in the hospital often asked if I knew who she was because she spent many hours visiting and assisting the men in the hospital.

Many thoughts ran through my head as I tried to figure out how this Marine could possibly know I knew her—and how could I tell him. Lucy had died many years earlier and I didn't know how to tell him. So I just said that I wasn't her but I knew her—and that she had died. And then I watched him tear up. After a moment he explained that she had written letters for him when he was wounded in the hospital in Danang—and he had come to DC on this Veterans Day weekend especially to see her. I told him that she had written a book about her experiences in Vietnam and I'd love to give him a copy. In fact, my parents were coming to DC the next day and could bring it, which they did, but although mother carried it around all Veterans Day, I was never able to connect them with him.

I saw him again at the women's dance and when I left, I knew I wouldn't see him again that visit, so I arranged to send the book to him. When I said good-bye, I kissed him on the cheek, something saved for special people under special circumstances.

I sent the book to him along with a note telling him how much I enjoyed meeting him and his crinkly eyes. He called me at the Friends of the Vietnam Veterans Memorial where I was volunteering to thank me, identifying himself as Ron XXXX. Having just met about 550 guys over Veterans Day, I had no idea who Ron XXXX was and so stumbled around until he said, "Crinkly Eyes." I knew immediately, and so our friendship continued.

Fast forward to a few years later. I'm talking to another veteran and I discover that he knows CE from a Vet Center group in California and that there's going to be a reunion of those folks soon. I tell him the story of our meeting—and then I have an idea.

I ask how he feels about kissing a Marine. He responds without hesitation, "No problem." So I ask him to find a time when there are lots of guys around and go up to Ron, kiss him on the check, and say, "Hi, Crinkly Eyes."

It was a great plan but CE foiled it by not showing up...that time....

A few years later when I was driving around the northwest, I stopped for a couple of days at Ron and Sue's. I had met Sue before, and it was nice to spend a little time with them both. One of their daughters said she hadn't seen him spend so much time out of the basement in ages.

And now he has died. Knowing him and his crinkly eyes makes me smile. I can't fathom not seeing them again.

Epilogue: The current owners of Lucy's house are also friends of my parents, and mine. At the entry of their home, there is a 3-tiered niche in the wall with shelves. On one of those shelves is Lucy's book which the current owners keep there because, as they say, it's a part of the house.

Lucy specified that the money from the sale of her book go to "a fund for the benefit of Marines permanently disabled in Vietnam." I find it particularly fitting that Lucy might have been thinking of my friend Ron when she made that donation.

China Beach

43

"China Beach" was a television series about women, mainly nurses, in Vietnam which ran from 1988-1991.

I visited the *China Beach* set because I had harassed Bill Broyles, one of the writers and a Vietnam veteran, by mail long enough that he arranged it. Bill was always very understanding and polite with me, always ending his letters with "Peace." I had told him that I felt like I had been betrayed by a fellow vet in his writing. My understanding, partly from him, partly from hearsay, partly from visiting the set, is that he had some control over it at first but in the second year had little to do with the program. Overall it was a pretty upsetting experience.

The portrayal of the Red Cross Donut Dollies in general was awful—very demeaning and untrue (for instance, we had to have college degrees and she didn't—not a big deal but an example; and they named her Cherry White—I wonder why). When I talked to co-writer John Sacret Young on the set, he professed to not understand the significance of Cherry White and why it was a problem. Neither of them seemed to be able to understand that we might be upset that KC, the woman of "loose morals," said she was a Donut Dollie before she quit to "do business."

Through the four years of the series I think the series sort of got better and those things were brushed over or forgotten by those who didn't care as much as we did. They continued to write really dumb things, like Cherry having her *Apocalypse Now* experience, but I guess I kind of came to terms with the fact that they at least included us and it wasn't too egregious.

While visiting the set, the actress who played Cherry was totally uninterested in talking to me. When I met her, the first thing I said to her was that she was wearing her name tag on the wrong side of her uniform. Not very tactful on my part, I admit, and she was cool to me afterwards. Probably would have been anyway since she was the "star."

There were two new "Donut Dollies" who were just joining the cast and were very excited to talk to me. I sat in their trailer for a while, showed them pictures and talked. They were supposed to be flying to their assignment that day and I told them how exciting an experience that had been for me. They were surprised because they thought we'd be scared and so, I guess, had been planning to portray it like that.

The only person other than the new DDs who was at all interested in acknowledging me was the man who played the doctor (he also played the hologram doctor on Star Trek). A real gentleman.

The filming experience itself was deadly—as Bill said, it's like watching grass grow. Everything moved so slowly—ages to set up a shot that lasted all of 30 seconds on screen. I'm glad I'm not an actor.

They had a Red Cross "advisor"—a Donut Dollie. It's hard to say how much influence she had—probably not much. Broyles, to his credit, did arrange in the second year to have a day or two of a Vietnam seminar wherein the actors, writers, etc. learned about Vietnam (finally). He also included a DD program, put on by real DDs. Apparently it went over very well, breaking the tension of so much intensity about Vietnam with fun and games— exactly what we set out to do in Vietnam. So they got a glimpse of what our purpose was. I highly doubt that it made any difference in the tone of the program.

I went to the *China Beach* website and started to write a comment. I got this far: "As a real-life Donut Dollie, the theme from *China Beach* can bring back waves of nostalgia—nostalgia for my tour in Vietnam and the bits and pieces of reality which CB managed to get right. On the other hand, it was painful to see what they got wrong," and then I ran out because I couldn't remember what they got wrong other than minor details. I guess I was so happy to see us finally recognized that I seem to have glossed over the bad.

The next year I was in DC when the cast came there over Veterans Day—Dana Delany, Troy Evans (a real Vietnam vet) and some others. Everyone was crowding around Delany at the hotel. I just watched. And then a vet I'd gotten to know through the years said to me, "She's just an actress. You're the real thing." Those who counted, knew.

It's All Vietnam

44

The Chilkoot

The Chilkoot Trail is the 33-mile route (mostly uphill) used during the Klondike gold rush in 1897-98 from Dyea, Alaska, to Lake Bennett, Canada. I climbed it, barely, in 1995 at age 52, and wrote about it to the veteran group.

Well, I did it, and I survived the Chilkoot, in spite of four blisters, a broken blood vessel in my knee, aching shoulders, and far too many years on my body. It was hard, real hard. 33 miles doesn't sound too bad, except that about 31 of those miles are either up or down and the few level miles (as well as the unlevel miles) have rocks the size of your fist or bigger in the trail so you can never really walk right, especially with blisters. The 3/4 of a mile of 45 degree angle took 2 1/2 hours of steady climbing on all fours over person-size and smaller boulders. It pushed me to my mental and physical limit—and I won!! And I will never do it again.

I've rappelled, jumped out of an airplane, hitchhiked through Morocco, soloed in a plane, owned a motorcycle, oh yeah, and been to Vietnam, twice— but this takes the cake.

Vietnam tie-in.

As you may know, I have always had the utmost respect and admiration for grunts. Now those feelings are profound. I thought a lot about you guys as I humped up and down—up and down a trail (not through the jungle or rice paddies), with a 40 (not 100) pound pack, in perfect weather with no bugs, with

Rangers waiting for us at the end instead of Charlie. As I thought about you, I realized that although I will of course never begin to understand what it was like for you, this was as close as I want to get to being pushed to that extent. And I also realized again, as I encountered two, count 'em 2, false summits, that you can keep going past what you thought was your limit—365 days plus.

The historical part was cool too. I have great admiration for the people who made the original climb, many times over, in the winter, with poor equipment—all for gold, and adventure. Maybe we have something in common....

Hospice

I've had an interesting month. I've been getting involved with the Hospice training and Big Brothers/Big Sisters. This has required me to tell people about my life on a more detailed and personal level than I usually do. So six times during the last month I've run through the death of my younger sister at age two, the death of my brother and the death of my mother two years ago. It's easy to write and easy to refer to in bits and controlled pieces. But every time I've recited my history during this month I've cried.

I think about death every day, I listen to you guys, I look at pictures of my brother and Mother on my walls, I think about my own death. Death is always with me. But I don't cry about it. So what the heck is going on with this now? The Hospice training is kicking my butt. I'm wiped out after nearly every session. My back is aching all the time.

It seems like grief never gets done, but of course I already knew that. It just keeps resurfacing, taking on different forms to ambush us again. I'm sick of it, and I think about walking away, tucking it back into the safer boxes where I've been keeping it. It's like those ghosts Michael talks about. I know they're out there—I just wish I knew how many more variations of them I'm going to have to deal with.

Twin Towers

When I was in New York with Red Cross disaster relief, I was able to spend about one hour during the late night at Ground Zero. It was, as everyone says, surrealistic. Lots of people walking around, with numerous food, cleaning, medical, respite spots. A strange smelling smoke pervaded the area (decontaminants have been sprayed on the pile so it's not a decomposing smell). I picked up a torn piece of paper that had recently blown off the pile which was a part of a woman's resume who had a computer background. I hoped she hadn't gotten the job.

During my hour at Ground Zero, I passed or briefly spoke to several workers. It reminded me of my early days in Vietnam and at the Wall when I was so unsure of myself about how to approach the men. Should I be solemn, smile, be neutral, make eye contact or not, nod or what. Some were quite cheerful, saying hi when they saw our Red Cross uniforms; others were less expressive. Since it was about three weeks after the event, the shock and urgency of their work had dissipated, so I'm sure the feeling was much lighter than it would have been earlier.

I didn't see the thousand-yard stare, but I know it was there.

Forrest Gump

Last week I was talking to the 13-year-old son of an old friend who has his sons for a few weeks in the summer. The boy lives in a small village and says he hasn't learned about Vietnam in school, and probably not much at home either. His father and I mentioned Vietnam in our conversation and the boy said to me, "Oh, that's right, you know about Vietnam." I allowed as how yes, I had a passing interest in it. He then asked, "Did America lose the war? I always hear how America lost the war but I don't know if that's right." I thought for a moment—how to explain to a kid, how to represent my thoughts and the various veterans' opinions, how to be fair. I then said, "America didn't achieve its objectives. In that sense we lost." We discussed it a little more, the French history, etc.

Then he asked, "Have you seen Forrest Gump?"

"Yes," I said.

"Was it realistic?"

"You mean the part about where they were running to the helicopter? Yes, that happened. I think it was pretty realistic and I've heard veterans say it was."

Then he said, "That's what the war was all about, wasn't it?"

I kind of started, wondering how he could have known that, if he really was saying what I thought he was, and asked what he meant.

"Guys trying to stay alive and keep their friends alive."

I said, "That's exactly what it was about. How did you know that?"

He had no answer, but what I came away from the conversation with was, first that he was one smart cookie, and second, that somehow, somewhere the word is getting through to some people.

M*A*S*H

In the 25 or so years that *M*A*S*H* has been on TV, I've watched it in various places at various times. One of the most memorable was when I worked for a local TV station here in Fairbanks. *M*A*S*H* was shown at a time when we did a live broadcast weekly, so we taped it, and every Friday afternoon after work, we'd drink beer, eat popcorn and watch the episode. Then for several years it was shown at 5:30, so I'd come home from work and relax as I watched it. Another time was one of the winters I spent in DC during the past few years. I had a late schedule, working until 10:00 pm or so, then I'd come home, eat dinner, and go to bed a couple of hours later. Two consecutive episodes of *M*A*S*H* were shown at midnight which I'd watch before I went to sleep.

I don't think I've seen a "new" show (one I haven't seen at least once and usually 4-5 times) in 10-15 years, but I still watch. It's like visiting with old friends, people I've known for years who have seen me through the good times and bad times, who are consistently interesting. And it's a piece of Vietnam.

It has just started again here, at 7:30, and I feel like my friends are back.

I Remember

45

I don't know when I wrote this—maybe around 2000. These are the moments and feelings that define Vietnam for me.

I remember Vietnam in pieces, in snapshots, soundbites. Not enough to write a story about or even a paragraph—but enough to fill up a lifetime.

I remember OJT—my first day on the job at An Khe. I went into the Red Cross recreation center via the back door into our office. I cracked the door to the main room and saw a sea of men in green and said, "I can't go out there." Donut 6 just said, "Come on." We walked over to a table of guys, she asked if we could sit with them, they said yes. They all chatted a few minutes together and then she got up and left me on my own. That was it. OJT.

I remember going to see my buddies the chopper mechanics after yet another mortar attack, checking on them because they lived near the airstrip. I saw the two of them walking toward me, one with a bandage on his forehead and the other who started limping badly, with a big smile on his face, as soon as he saw me.

I remember sitting in a bunker taping a message home to my parents—in the bunker because it was the only private place, but starting the tape with sounds of outgoing mortars, just for the sake of drama.

I remember that I always found out what the officers were like by asking their men. With one platoon I made a joke about how young their lieutenant looked, got sour responses, and realized that these men didn't take to any girl making cracks about their LT.

I remember hearing about a Donut Dollie who kept her bottom drawer full of flashcards with swear words on them which she would open up and read when she'd been pushed to the limit. She always ended up laughing.

I remember the sign in the Freedom Hill recreation center in Danang, the sign with the sayings on it which we changed weekly. This week it said, "What would men do without women? Lots of push-ups."

I remember the burn victim in the NSA hospital—the one the nurse asked me to go talk to—completely bandaged, unable to speak. I tried talking for a minute or two, gave up in desperation and asked another Donut Dollie to do it for me.

I remember wishing I could go home and wishing I could stay. I remember being so sick of GIs I never wanted to see another, and then being the first one to volunteer for an extra run.

I remember going to an Aussie unit and "swimming" in a child's play pool while drinking a beer.

I remember sitting around one evening in Tay Ninh while a guy played the guitar and sang each and every song anyone had ever heard of, with all the verses.

I remember going into a bunker on a firebase where the guys didn't want me, were uncomfortable having me there. I was never quite sure why—it was something specific, something they'd been saying or doing that didn't want a woman. I don't know why, but I remember it and it's okay.

I remember playing liar's dice, hour after hour, in the officers' club at Cu Chi—a way to hang with something to do.

I remember the guys at the R&R unit (our nickname for Radio Research) getting such a charge out of my frequent visits to their unit because of my obvious interest in one of their guys—a blond boy with a slow southern drawl.

I remember getting sour looks from the 25th Infantry guys when I pinned a screaming eagle patch on my uniform to welcome a brigade of the 101st to Cu Chi.

I remember our old Vietnamese mama-san in Danang who told me not to leave my money lying around because the other hooch maid would take it.

I remember the peace of flying in the choppers—being away from everyone with nothing to do except sit there and be a part of the sky.

I remember hating the war, and knowing that I'd never be that good again.

I don't remember wondering what it would be like back in the world. I don't remember wondering what my life would be like afterwards. I don't remember thinking I'd never be the same, although I must have realized that.

I remember saying to a Donut Dollie friend halfway through my tour, "This will be the best year of my life." I was right.

Vietnam — 1 Year + 25

46

One year I was going through my Vietnam papers (I saved every-thing written about Vietnam for years) when I came across something in my handwriting. I didn't remember writing it, but I figured I must have written it in 1993 because of the title—1968 + 25 = 1993.

How do you sum up Vietnam in a few paragraphs? Vietnam isn't just the one year spent in country, but it's also the 25 years since we got back.

Vietnam isn't just a country in Southeast Asia where we spent a year of our lives. For many of us, it is our lives.

Vietnam isn't just an interlude in our growing up—a stage be-tween adolescence and adulthood. Vietnam is our childhood, our adolescence, our adulthood, our old age, and for some of us, our death.

Vietnam isn't just a time period when we were learning new things about ourselves and our lives. Vietnam is the 1 year plus 25 when we learned more than we could ever understand about our-selves and life and death.

Vietnam isn't just a year when our lives were on hold. Vietnam is the peak experience of our lives, the touchstone by which we test every other experience, every other relationship, every other high, every other low.

Vietnam is a blessing and a curse, our life and our death, our creation and our destruction, a soaring and a drowning, our true love and our hated enemy, an R&R and a firefight, a freedom bird and an ambush.

We'd probably do it again, given a chance, but we wouldn't want our kids to.

Vietnam gave us who we are, and keeps trying to take it away. It gave us who we are, and won't let us be who we want to be.

Vietnam is hundreds of young men smiling, and hundreds of older men crying.

Vietnam is a girl finally coming into her own, and a woman still looking for the girl.

Vietnam is when we learned to love not just the people we knew, but the ones we would never meet.

Vietnam is an abiding love for the men who only ever needed to smile at us to make that 1 year + 25 all worth it.

Afterword

47

I have lived with Vietnam for 50+ years. I've lived with the death of my brother and the effect it's had on my family and their friends and his friends.

A death is like throwing a rock into a quiet lake. The ripples from that one rock extend out in all directions, causing a disturbance as far as it goes. One of the forms that ripple took for me was to first lead me to despair, to a lack of hope for a better mankind and world. It took away any latent belief I might have had in God because he didn't appear to care about the plight of those inhabitants of the world.

Then I actually looked at what the Bible says about his plan—simply the fact that he has a plan—a plan where there is no more death and people will live forever on the earth in peace. Learning that Jehovah God actually does care about us and that it pains him to see us suffer gave me a new outlook on life. It gave me hope.

So Vietnam will always be with me. It has shaped me—it's taken from me but it has also given me much. I've come to know people I never would have met otherwise. Through sharing others' pain I've grown in understanding and compassion. I've learned to forgive a nation that wasn't at fault. I've learned the benefit of dark humor—that you can laugh at pain. It's given me a depth of caring, of belonging I hadn't felt before.

I would trade it all to have my brother back.

I look forward to the time when Vietnam will still be a memory, but a memory without the pain, the sting. It will be a time when I can be with my brother again and together we can hear the stories of the many others who did not survive the war, either in Vietnam or at home. It will be a time of peace at last.

Appendix

Letters about Billy

From the letter of a father to his children, one of them a girl Billy had dated in high school:

"As I walked up to the steps of the church about 10 minutes before 11, there were perhaps a hundred people lined up on the steps and on the street waiting in line to sign an [attendance] book."

[continuing the father's letter] "Certainly I think he was the finest young man who ever visited our home, and I'll never forget the evening, Deb, that you and Bill were delayed by the car breakdown and arrived home in the wee hours. As a parent, it was a warm experience at the time to see how he handled himself."

From the talk at the service by his 3-year college roommate:

"We all know Billy as a happy-go-lucky guy who brought smiles and laughter. Further we know the athlete that got on the ice, did his job, and got off. And more, there was a quiet concern to understand the people and the life he was so significantly a part of. His sense of humor, his competitiveness and selfless approach to people came together in Bill's courage to do a job."

From a teacher or administrator at prep school:

"As you know, I knew Bill in many areas and was never disappointed in any of them. There are few, if any, of the many people who have gone through this school of whom I was as fond and whom I admired as much."

From a math teacher at prep school:

"During his senior year hardly a day passed that he did not stop in at my office where we had lots of laughs as well as serious thoughts. [At the 5th reunion of the class] Bill appointed himself a committee of one to fetch me out at my home where we had a really great visit for a couple of hours. I could not help but be impressed with his whole attitude toward life and the world in general. He was certainly more understanding of the current situation than I was, and after this tragedy, am now."

From the friend of the younger sister of a prep school friend, written in 1993:

"I knew him only slightly as the wonderful friend of the Meck family.... Julie and I enjoyed going to the games, and after soccer games, Bill would always come over to say hello and talk to us. This made us feel special, and together with the interest he showed in what we had to say, are what leave me, even today, with the impression of kindness and thoughtfulness. We were all cheated when he was not able to enrich the world through a longer life. I just wanted you to know, I'll always remember the fine son you raised."

From a college friend:

"Bill did not permit his excellence and his promise to overcome personal warmth. Seemingly unaffected by his excellence and promise, Bill opened himself to those without any near combination of his qualities. Bill was a warm person, a person who didn't try to make others over in his own image, but rather a person who accepted people for what they were, and liked them for it. Almost unconsciously, Bill made friends with faculty members and students, with Mid-westerners and Easterners, with athletes and non-athletes, with failing students and Rhodes scholars, with handsome people and homely people, with broad-minded people and narrow-minded people.... In times of achievement he was humble in bestowing his greatness upon his friends. In times of failure or sorrow, he strived for the better..."

One of his college friends who is now a well-known producer/ director on Broadway recently told us that what he remembers most about Billy is how Billy used to go out of his way to speak warmly to him even though he (the director) was a self-described nerd at the time.

From a soccer referee at college:

"I have never seen anyone who embodied my ideas of the perfect athlete and gentleman more than did Billy. I will never forget his greeting to me before every game, words to the effect that it's good to see you again, Mr. Williams. I'll never forget those rare times when Bill felt I missed a call and would quietly say, 'Ref, I think you missed it' in such a way that you knew he had to believe it was a bad call and not an excuse for himself or his teammates. Also, I'll treasure those moments after a game, regardless of whether Dartmouth won or lost, when he'd come up, shake my hand, and say, 'Great game, Mr. Williams,' and would ask me what games I had coming up."

From the custodian of his freshman dorm at college:

"I found him to be one of the finest boys and one that was well worthwhile knowing and both my wife and I will always be glad we knew him. Even after I retired he took time to visit me now and then."

From a college friend, 2 years younger:

"I remember the time he would take to help me and others in soccer, hockey and rugby. He went out of his way to coach and encourage underclassmen. He was also the type of guy who you had to stand in awe of until you met him. For all his capabilities and campus status, there was no one more humble or more outgoing. Everyone who knew Bill loved him."

From one of his best friends at college, written in 1978:

"I must say that the immense feeling of loss experienced has not diminished after 10 full years. Bill's memory stays strongly with me—and I am very thankful for that.... My old friends are still my best friends. Ten years ago I lost a lifetime friend and the pain still exists because he cannot be replaced."

From a college friend, written in 1990:

"It is funny, but I think you will understand when I tell you that I have often been surprised to find myself remembering Bill at odd times. He had a sense of humor I found particularly appealing, a way of making you slightly uncomfortable, until you realized what he was doing and in that realization you learned something about yourself. I remember him as a vital man, charged with happy energy, a good sportsman, someone who loved people and did not seem afraid of life, someone who made you glad when he came into a room. I remember, too, what I thought of as his increasing uncertainty about that damned war as our last year grew shorter."

From the program for a Dartmouth hockey game at which a lounge in the new hockey rink was dedicated in Billy's name:

It was 1966 and the soccer team traveled by plane to Cornell. "For Bill, this was a problem. He hated to fly. True to form, Smoyer had bouts with air sickness before the plane touched down in Ithaca. The next morning he was still under the weather and unable to eat.... With 30 seconds to play in the match, Cornell led, 2-1. On the sideline, [the coach] was reconciled to defeat when Smoyer's shot from 25 yards out sent the game into overtime. Play in the overtime period was scoreless into the last minutes...when Smoyer altered the inevitable.., with a shot from much the same spot as the tying goal. Despite his achievements, Smoyer kept a low profile among his teammates and fellow students. He was totally respected and liked."

From the soccer coach in a letter to me in 1990:

"No one made such an indelible mark on my own life as did Billy. In a way, I still have trouble believing in the reality of the situation. The conclusion that I finally reached was, quite simply, that I guess I thought Billy was invincible. I never saw him in a stressful situation that he couldn't handle.... He never panicked, never flustered. He could always think and work his way out. He could operate in disaster and finish in style. He had class. He was exceptional.

"However, he was operating in situations where the behavioral patterns of his opponents were fairly predictable and both sides were governed by the same set of rules.... [In Vietnam there were] imposed restrictions on how you are to play the game against an opponent who has no such regulations and suddenly the playing field is not very level.

"I have used the following many times when talking to young people concerning their future as leaders.

"As a leader,
1. You can command a man's time.
2. You can command a man's physical presence in a given place.
3. You can command a measured number of skilled muscular motions per hour or day.

"But...
1. You cannot command enthusiasm.
2. You cannot command initiative.
3. You cannot command loyalty.
4. You cannot command devotion or hearts, minds and souls.

These things you have to earn!

"The young men who looked to Billy for leadership had no difficulty with the last found ingredients. He had charisma. He was believable. He was inspirational. He made you want to be part of whatever it was he was doing."

Acknowledgments

First and foremost I want to thank the GIs in Vietnam and the veterans I've come to know afterwards. They formed me and my life. They tried to figure out the unique role of the Donut Dollies while we were in Vietnam, and later have understood that we share a common experience, both in Vietnam and in the aftermath. With some hesitation, on both our parts, we have come to a deep appreciation and caring which continues to grow as we age together, sharing our memories.

Many of the Donut Dollies with whom I shared this journey, albeit in our individual ways, I met after the war at Donut Dollie reunions and gatherings at the Wall. I love the memories I have of the girls I knew in Vietnam and of the women with whom I've become friends. Every story I hear from them increases my own experience and the knowledge that we were a special group of 627 girls in an amazing situation.

I've had a lot of help from friends—civilian and veteran—dating back many years of hearing people tell me, "You should write a book." When I finally did get it on paper, my "readers" offered encouragement as I tried to figure out whether the format of combining letters and emails was coherent and whether it held people's interest. Two people were particularly important because they hung in through many readings and offering of suggestions throughout the process. One is my ever-loyal sister-in-law and friend, Mary Howland Smoyer, married to my older brother, David. The other is Robert Doubek, co-founder of the Vietnam Veterans Memorial Fund and author of *Creating the Vietnam Veterans Memorial: The Inside Story*. Then when I despaired of ever getting it published in the format I wanted, I turned to Ray Bonnell who offered advice and practical expertise as a publication consultant to produce a finished product.

My parents shaped me to be adventurous and I succeeded beyond their wishes. Although they are no longer with us, I owe a debt of gratitude to them for not putting up blockades and for accepting my adventures with grace. Vietnam was painful for them in so many ways, but they never questioned or asked me to "let it go" any more than they could.

Made in the USA
Monee, IL
16 March 2025

14062885R00138